GO & MULTIPLY

SHARING THE GOSPEL IN WORD AND DEED

devoted
Discipleship Training for Small Groups

Go & Multiply: Sharing the Gospel In Word and Deed

Devoted: Discipleship Training for Small Groups

Copyright © 2019 by Clear Creek Community Church and Yancey Arrington

Editorial Team: Mandy Turner, Ryan Lehtinen, Jon Coffey

Published by Clear Creek Resources

A Ministry of Clear Creek Community Church

999 North FM 270

League City, Texas 77573

ISBN: 978-0-9979469-5-6

Printed in the United States of America

CONTENTS

INTRODUCTION

You are a missionary. You may not have thought of yourself as one, but if you're a follower of Jesus it's true.

This study is designed to train you to be a missionary who has been sent by your Savior to go and multiply.

Since its founding, Clear Creek Community Church has had one mission: to lead unchurched people to become fully devoted followers of Jesus Christ. This mission is simply a modern restating of Jesus' words in Matthew 28:19-20 whereby he commissioned his followers to "make disciples" of the world around them. In essence, Christ shows us what a Christian is to be – a disciple who makes disciples. This is the purpose behind the Devoted: Descipleship Training for Small Groups series. It is based upon the gospel truths explained in the Spiritual Growth Grid:

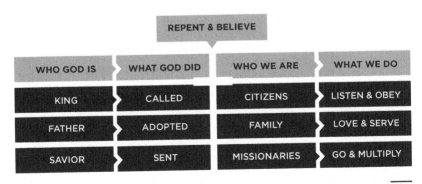

This study is part of the Go & Multiply storyline. Over the next 10 weeks, you will learn key concepts about the gospel identity of missionaries and how you are sent to go and multiply through sharing the gospel in word and deed. You will be trained to engage in missional prayer, to be a missional presence, and to share your grace story with missional proclamation. All of it tethered to the gospel storyline that God is our Savior who, as he sent Christ to redeem us, also sends us as missionaries to go and multiply!

May the Lord use this in his grace to make us disciple-making disciples.

Grace to you,
The Elders of Clear Creek Community Church

USING THE STUDY

Devoted is a two-year small group study series focused on training in the essentials of being a disciple who makes disciples. It is designed to help small groups grow deeper in the concepts of the Spiritual Growth Grid. This means, regardless of where you are on the spiritual journey, you play your part in the group each week when you:

Step 1: Memorize the Scripture

Throughout the study you will memorize key Bible passages specifically chosen for the topic. Practice reciting these each day. Try to fill in the blank spaces from memory as you prepare to recite the passages at your next small group meeting.

Step 2: Study the Scripture

The Bible passages are chosen because of the study's general theme. They are good Scriptures to know as either citizens, family, or missionaries. They don't necessarily relate directly to the day's teaching. This is a section where we want disciples to grow in the skill of observing and interpreting a text. The teaching that follows will deal with biblical application.

Step 3: Read the Teaching

Take your time to read through the day's teaching. The questions that follow are designed to help you better process the lesson in light of the Spiritual Growth Grid and apply the principles. Afterwards, take time to pray using the prompts provided.

Step 4: Do the Weekly Exercise

You will find a weekly exercise at the end of each week's Day 3 material. The exercises often employ different learning styles to practice the principles been taught. Be sure to not only do the exercise but the reflection section as well. The exercises are intended to help build your skill set as a disciple-making disciple.

Step 5: Ready Yourself for Group

The last section of each week's material concludes with the *Get Ready for Group* section. This allows you to summarize your key takeaways for the week in preparation for small group discussion. Please be sure to answer the final question concerning how the week's lessons help you better integrate the Spiritual Growth Grid. This will help your Navigator identify possible areas of further study in order to better live out one's gospel identity. Remember, the point is to be trained to be a disciple who makes disciples!

01

UNDERSTANDING THE GOSPEL

SCRIPTURE MEMORY

Therefore, we are ambassadors for Christ, God making his appeal through us. We implore you on behalf of Christ, be reconciled to God.

—2 Corinthians 5:20

THE GOSPEL OVER TIME

Scripture Study

2 CORINTHIANS 5:11-17

Therefore, knowing the fear of the Lord, we persuade others. But what we are is known to God, and I hope it is known also to your conscience. [12] We are not commending ourselves to you again but giving you cause to boast about us, so that you may be able to answer those who boast about outward appearance and not about what is in the heart. [13] For if we are beside ourselves, it is for God; if we are in our right mind, it is for you. [14] For the love of Christ controls us, because we have concluded this: that one has died for all, therefore all have died; [15] and he died for all, that those who live might no longer live for themselves but for him who for their sake died and was raised. [16] From now on, therefore, we regard no one according to the flesh. Even though we once regarded Christ according to the flesh, we regard him thus no longer. [17] Therefore, if anyone is in Christ, he is a new creation. The old has passed away; behold, the new has come.

Observing the Text

For whose sake did Christ die and rise again?

_____

_____

What is the impact of his death on the life of those who live?

_____

_____

_____

What is the result of being "in Christ"?

_____

_____

_____

Interpreting the Text

What does Paul mean when he says "one has died for all, therefore all have died" but then "he died for all, that those who live might no longer live for themselves..."? How can we "all have died" but there are still "those who live"?

_____

_____

_____

What does it mean to be "in Christ"? What might that look like?

_____

_____

_____

Why does Paul use the phrase "a new creation" to describe those who are in Christ?

_____

_____

_____

Teaching

Everyone has a story, including God himself. His is the story of history. You can summarize that story in four movements:

CREATION – FALL – REDEMPTION – RESTORATION

God created the world as a paradise, and placed humanity (specifically Adam and Eve) as the crowning glory of it all. God chose mankind to have a special relationship with him by enjoying his goodness and stewarding his perfect creation. God's kingdom, his perfect reign and rule, was in full effect.

But we blew it.

Given the chance to follow God or our own ways, our representatives Adam and Eve chose rebellion; as a result, the cosmos suffered a great fall. Sin entered the picture. Consequently, God's perfect creation was deeply broken. Nothing remained untouched by the ugliness of sin—marriage, family, work, community, etc. Humanity was left with strife in how people related to creation, each other, and most of all, God. His perfect holiness demanded that humanity's rebellion be dealt with in perfect justice. Thus, because of the Fall, mankind stood condemned under the judgment and wrath of God. Paradise was lost.

But God, in his great love and mercy, promised to send a Rescuer who through his person and work would provide redemption for his creation. Two thousand years ago, that Redeemer arrived in the person of Jesus Christ.

Jesus, both fully God and fully human, entered humanity's mess by joining us in it—breathing the air we breathe, drinking the water we drink, living like one of us. Yet, unlike us, Jesus never sinned. He faultlessly obeyed God's law, thus meriting entrance into God's kingdom by his perfection. Jesus did what we should have done but could not do.

Christ then became our substitute by taking our punishment for sin on a cross. God the Father poured out upon Jesus his just wrath that we deserved. We receive Christ's perfect righteousness in return for placing our faith and trust in him alone for salvation. Jesus' resurrection three days later proclaimed his victory over sin, death, and hell! Through the person and work of Jesus, sinners can be fully and eternally redeemed back to God and his kingdom. It is this tale of redemption through God's grace in Jesus—not by anything we have done—we call the "Gospel."

The gospel is good news that changes everything! Truly everything. A day is coming when Christ will return and bring restoration, returning creation to its original state of perfection. At his return, Jesus will wipe the universe clean of sin, sickness, disease—even death itself. Paradise lost becomes paradise restored. The kingdom of God will reign on the earth in its fullness. God will dwell with his people like he did before, in perfect peace and fellowship.

This is the story of history—it's creation, fall, redemption, and restoration. This is the story of God. And now, through your redemption by the grace of God in Christ, you have been included in his story.

Knowing the story helps us understand the state of our world and where history is ultimately headed—a time when everything will once again be under God's rule and reign. It also shows us how God wants to use his people for the sake of his kingdom. We are sent out to tell others about the redemption we've found in Jesus.

Questions for Reflection

What does it mean that our salvation was accomplished through the person and work of Jesus?

_____

_____

_____

How has the gospel changed your life—your relationships, your choices, your priorities?

_____

_____

_____

In what ways have you failed to appreciate the majesty of God's work on behalf of humanity? What new habits could you create in order to appreciate this Good News and trust in it more deeply?

_____

_____

_____

Prayer

Thank God for his work in accomplishing the redemption of humanity through the sacrifice of his Son. Pray that he would increase your understanding of his great work of salvation, resulting in his glory and your growth.

SCRIPTURE MEMORY

Therefore, we are _____ for Christ, God making his appeal through us. We implore you on behalf of Christ, be _____ to God.

—*2 Corinthians 5:20*

THE GOSPEL IN TIME

Scripture Study

2 CORINTHIANS 5:11-17

Therefore, knowing the fear of the Lord, we persuade others. But what we are is known to God, and I hope it is known also to your conscience. [12] We are not commending ourselves to you again but giving you cause to boast about us, so that you may be able to answer those who boast about outward appearance and not about what is in the heart. [13] For if we are beside ourselves, it is for God; if we are in our right mind, it is for you. [14] For the love of Christ controls us, because we have concluded this: that one has died for all, therefore all have died; [15] and he died for all, that those who live might no longer live for themselves but for him who for their sake died and was raised. [16] From now on, therefore, we regard no one according to the flesh. Even though we once regarded Christ according to the flesh, we regard him thus no longer. [17] Therefore, if anyone is in Christ, he is a new creation. The old has passed away; behold, the new has come.

Observing the text

Who knows Paul's identity, even if others perceive it inaccurately?

_____

_____

What is the defining attribute of Christ in this passage that controls Paul and those with him?

_____

_____

_____

In what way has Paul's regard for Christ changed?

_____

_____

_____

Interpreting the text

What does Paul know that leads him to persuade others? Why does this matter?

_____

_____

_____

What does it mean that they "regarded Christ according to the flesh," but no longer do?

_____

_____

_____

What does the "new creation" of anyone who is in Christ imply about their former state?

_____

_____

_____

Teaching

The gospel can be spoken about in two ways: *over time* and *in time*. The last lesson presented the full historical scope of what God is doing in Christ (*over time*). This lesson focuses on our personal interaction with the gospel (*in time*). The first way of presenting the gospel illustrates God's movement through all history; the second way deals specifically with our engagement with God in Christ through our personal history.

The gospel *in time* can be summarized in four words[1]:

GOD – MAN – CHRIST – RESPONSE

GOD
God is the creator of all things and made us in his image to know him. He is perfectly holy, worthy of all worship, and will punish sin. (Genesis 1:1; Genesis 1:26-28; 1 John 1:5; Revelation 4:11; Romans 2:5-8)

MAN
All people, though created good, have become sinful by nature and by choice. As a result, all people are alienated from God, hostile to God, and subject to the wrath of God. (Genesis 1:26-28; Psalm 51:5; Romans 2:4-6, 3:23; Revelation 20:12; Ephesians 2:1-3)

CHRIST
In his great love, God became a man in Jesus, lived a perfect life, and died on the cross, thus fulfilling the law himself and taking on himself the punishment for the sins of all those who would ever turn and trust in him. He rose from the dead, showing that

---

1 Adapted from Mark Dever's book *The Gospel and Personal Evangelism*

God accepted Christ's sacrifice and that God's wrath against us had been exhausted. (John 1:1; 1 Timothy 2:5; Hebrews 7:26; Romans 3:21-26; 2 Corinthians 5:21; 1 Corinthians 15:20-22)

RESPONSE | God now calls us to repent of our sins and to trust in Christ alone for our forgiveness. If we repent of our sins and trust in Jesus, we are born again into a new life—an eternal life with God. (Mark 1:15; Acts 20:21; Romans 10:9-10)

Talking about the gospel *in time* is one effective way to understand the gospel. The focus isn't on God's work throughout history but instead how the good news intersects our personal history. Throughout this entire study we will see how both ways of understanding the gospel can help us better share it through our words and deeds.

Questions for Reflection
How has this second method of understanding the gospel amplified your understanding of God's work of redemption?

_____

_____

_____

In what ways does our cultural mindset contrast with the view of humanity inherent in the gospel, attempting to deny the truth of our sin?

_____

_____

_____

Which of these two ways of understanding the gospel is most familiar to you? In what way is each of them helpful?

_____

_____

Prayer

Praise God for his perfection in all things and the grace he showed in choosing to enter into humanity himself in response to our rebellion. Thank him specifically for how he showed himself to you so that you could respond by faith.

SCRIPTURE MEMORY

_____, we are ambassadors for Christ, ____ making his appeal through us. We implore you on behalf of Christ, be reconciled to ____.

—*2 Corinthians 5:20*

GOOD NEWS NOT GOOD ADVICE

Scripture Study

2 CORINTHIANS 5:11-17

Therefore, knowing the fear of the Lord, we persuade others. But what we are is known to God, and I hope it is known also to your conscience. [12] We are not commending ourselves to you again but giving you cause to boast about us, so that you may be able to answer those who boast about outward appearance and not about what is in the heart. [13] For if we are beside ourselves, it is for God; if we are in our right mind, it is for you. [14] For the love of Christ controls us, because we have concluded this: that one has died for all, therefore all have died; [15] and he died for all, that those who live might no longer live for themselves but for him who for their sake died and was raised.[16] From now on, therefore, we regard no one according to the flesh. Even though we once regarded Christ according to the flesh, we regard him thus no longer. [17] Therefore, if anyone is in Christ, he is a new creation. The old has passed away; behold, the new has come.

Observing the Text

What does Paul say is worth boasting about: outward appearance or the contents of the heart?

_____

_____

_____

In this passage, what are the effects of Christ's death for all?

_____

_____

_____

For whom do believers now live, and for whom do we no longer live?

_____

_____

_____

Interpreting the Text

Is Paul controlled by the love OF Christ or his love FOR Christ? Why does this matter?

_____

_____

_____

What does it mean to not live for ourselves but for the one who died for us?

_____

_____

_____

If those who are in Christ are new creations, are they the active party in bringing about this creation? Why does this matter?

_____

Teaching

No matter how we present it we must realize the gospel never changes—it is always the good news of God's grace in Jesus on our behalf.

Look at how the apostle Paul reacts when he hears about how some Galatian Christians were considering leaving the good news of grace in Jesus for a "faith of advice" where one would have to perform for God's acceptance. Paul says in Galatians 1:6-9:

> I am astonished that you are so quickly deserting him who called you in the grace of Christ and are turning to a different gospel—not that there is another one, but there are some who trouble you and want to distort the gospel of Christ. But even if we or an angel from heaven should preach to you a gospel contrary to the one we preached to you, let him be accursed. As we have said before, so now I say again: If anyone is preaching to you a gospel contrary to the one you received, let him be accursed.

False teachers were saying, "I know you've embraced Jesus' death on the Cross for you, but God will only accept you if you get circumcised, attend this feast, adopt these customs, etc." Essentially they were teaching what people needed to do *in addition to faith in Christ* for God to accept them. But, Paul asserts that this addition nullifies the gospel itself—it's not good news anymore.

When the gospel becomes advice (i.e., what we need to do for God) it's not the gospel anymore. The moment you believe that God's acceptance of you is based on how well you perform and obey, you're not believing the gospel. The message of salvation says Christ alone has achieved our acceptance with God. This gospel is rooted in the good news that God in Christ has accomplished what we never could.

When someone objects, saying, "No, you need Jesus plus [INSERT: good works, religious deeds, etc.]," they are not giving you good news but merely advice. There is a big difference between good news and good advice. The gospel is the former and never the latter.

The gospel is also unique in that if you try to add to it, you actually subtract from it—winding up with something less than the gospel. We can never change the gospel because the gospel never changes.

We understand the gospel well when we trust that it was, is, and always will be about God doing for us in Christ what we cannot do for ourselves.

Questions for Reflection

Is it surprising to you that pollution of the true gospel was already occurring so early in the life of the church? What does it say about human nature that this happened then and is still going on today?

_____

_____

_____

What are some examples of requirements that you hear added to the gospel within our Christian culture? Which of these have you struggled with?

_____

_____

_____

What are ways that we can fight for the integrity of the gospel in the way we speak to each other at group and in the world?

_____

_____

_____

Prayer

Ask God to show you how you are seeking to earn his acceptance rather than resting in the promise that your salvation has already been accomplished for you. Thank him for his perfect life and sacrifice that did what would have been impossible on your own.

WEEKLY
EXERCISE

ARTICULATING THE GOSPEL

Take some time throughout this week and write out how you would articulate the gospel in your own words. Challenge yourself to share it as both the gospel "over time" and "in time." Think through using the movements mentioned in this week's teaching sections. Try to include Scripture references. Feel free to do this exercise on a separate sheet of paper.

Get Ready for Group

Write your memorized Scripture.

_____

_____

_____

_____

_____

What observations and interpretations of Scripture were most meaningful to you?

_____

_____

_____

_____

_____

Summarize your key takeaway(s) for this week.

_____

_____

_____

_____

_____

What will you tell the group about the results of your exercise this week?

_____

_____

_____

_____

_____

How has this week helped you better understand and apply the Spiritual Growth Grid?

_____

_____

_____

_____

_____

REPENT & BELIEVE

WHO GOD IS	WHAT GOD DID	WHO WE ARE	WHAT WE DO
KING	CALLED	CITIZENS	LISTEN & OBEY
FATHER	ADOPTED	FAMILY	LOVE & SERVE
SAVIOR	SENT	MISSIONARIES	GO & MULTIPLY

02

OUR MISSIONARY IDENTITY

SCRIPTURE MEMORY

Therefore, we are ambassadors for Christ, God making his appeal through us. We implore you on behalf of Christ, be reconciled to God.

—2 Corinthians 5:20

OUR SENDING GOD

Scripture Study

2 CORINTHIANS 5:11-21

Therefore, knowing the fear of the Lord, we persuade others. But what we are is known to God, and I hope it is known also to your conscience. [12] We are not commending ourselves to you again but giving you cause to boast about us, so that you may be able to answer those who boast about outward appearance and not about what is in the heart. [13] For if we are beside ourselves, it is for God; if we are in our right mind, it is for you. [14] For the love of Christ controls us, because we have concluded this: that one has died for all, therefore all have died; [15] and he died for all, that those who live might no longer live for themselves but for him who for their sake died and was raised.

[16] From now on, therefore, we regard no one according to the flesh. Even though we once regarded Christ according to the flesh, we regard him thus no longer. [17] Therefore, if anyone is in Christ, he is a new creation. The old has passed away; behold, the new has come. [18] All this is from God, who through Christ reconciled us to himself and gave us the ministry of reconciliation; [19] that is, in Christ God was reconciling the world to himself, not counting their trespasses against them, and entrusting to us the message of reconciliation. [20] Therefore, we are ambassadors for Christ, God making

his appeal through us. We implore you on behalf of Christ, be reconciled to God. [21] For our sake he made him to be sin who knew no sin, so that in him we might become the righteousness of God.

Observing the Text (verses 18-21)

What did God do to us through Christ?

_____

_____

_____

What ministry and message did he then give us?

_____

_____

_____

What is God no longer counting against those who have been reconciled?

_____

_____

_____

Interpreting the Text (verses 18-21)

How would you define reconciliation as used in this passage?

_____

_____

_____

Why is "not counting their trespasses against them" a necessary part of reconciliation?

_____

_____

_____

Who was reconciled to God and to whom was given the ministry of reconciliation? What is implied by the use of the same pronoun?

_____

_____

_____

Teaching

Titus 3:4-6 reads:

> But when the goodness and loving kindness of God our Savior
> appeared, he saved us, not because of works done by us in
> righteousness, but according to his own mercy, by the wash-
> ing of regeneration and renewal of the Holy Spirit, whom he
> poured out on us richly through Jesus Christ our Savior.

Hundreds of times in the Bible, God either is called Savior or speaks of saving his people. What do we need to be saved from? In Matthew 1:21, Joseph heard an angel proclaim, "She [Mary] will bear a son, and you shall call his name Jesus, for he will save his people from their sins."

The cross was God's plan to sacrifice his Son to rescue us from the penalty and consequences of our sins. The work of God through his Son redeems us because sin enslaved us, reconciles us because sin separated us, justifies us because sin condemned us, and restores us because sin shattered our lives.

God's act of grace in response to our sin is the heart of the gospel. It's the essential truth all our beliefs are founded upon. But it isn't the end of the story. When Jesus appeared to his disciples following his resurrection, he didn't just enjoy their company, he gave them a mission.

Jesus said to them again, "Peace be with you. As the Father has sent me, even so I am sending you."

John 20:21

God sent Jesus to be our Savior, but God was not finished sending. As followers of Jesus, we are sent into our world to show people that God has come to redeem and restore all people and, ultimately, all of creation back to God. Our next lesson will further delve into the implications of what it means to be sent.

Questions for Reflection

In what ways does our nature fight against the idea that we need to be saved? How does our culture discourage us from admitting our need for a Savior?

_____

_____

_____

Why does it matter that God identifies himself as a Savior? What does that display about his character?

_____

_____

_____

How can you speak and act within your small groups in a way that acknowledges and celebrates your need for a Savior and God's act of salvation on your behalf?

_____

_____

_____

Prayer

Thank Jesus today for both who he is and what he has done.

SCRIPTURE MEMORY

Therefore, we are ambassadors for Christ, God making his _____ through us. We _____ you on behalf of _____, be reconciled to God.

—2 Corinthians 5:20

OUR GOSPEL IDENTITY: MISSIONARIES

Scripture Study

2 CORINTHIANS 5:11-21

Therefore, knowing the fear of the Lord, we persuade others. But what we are is known to God, and I hope it is known also to your conscience. ¹² We are not commending ourselves to you again but giving you cause to boast about us, so that you may be able to answer those who boast about outward appearance and not about what is in the heart. ¹³ For if we are beside ourselves, it is for God; if we are in our right mind, it is for you. ¹⁴ For the love of Christ controls us, because we have concluded this: that one has died for all, therefore all have died; ¹⁵ and he died for all, that those who live might no longer live for themselves but for him who for their sake died and was raised.

¹⁶ From now on, therefore, we regard no one according to the flesh. Even though we once regarded Christ according to the flesh, we regard him thus no longer. ¹⁷ Therefore, if anyone is in Christ, he is a new creation. The old has passed away; behold, the new has come. ¹⁸ All this is from God, who through Christ reconciled us to himself and gave us the ministry of reconciliation; ¹⁹ that is, in Christ God was reconciling the world to himself, not counting their trespasses against them, and entrusting to us the message of reconciliation. [20] Therefore, we are ambassadors for Christ, God making his appeal through us. We implore you on behalf of Christ, be reconciled to God. [21] For our sake he made him to be sin who knew no sin, so that in him we might become the righteousness of God.

Observing the text (verses 18-21)

What title is given to those whom God is making his appeal through?

_____

_____

_____

What appeal is God making?

_____

_____

_____

On whose behalf are we asking others to be reconciled?

_____

_____

_____

Interpreting the text (verses 18-21)

What does it mean to be an ambassador? What responsibilities does that imply?

_____

_____

_____

Why does it matter that the message of reconciliation has been "entrusted" to us?

_____

_____

_____

Why would God do the work of reconciliation through Christ but then entrust the message to us? What does it then mean when Paul claims to "implore [others] on behalf of Christ"?

_____

_____

_____

Teaching

We noted in our last study that God sent Jesus to be our Savior, but God was not finished sending. As disciples of Jesus, we also are sent into the world to proclaim that God has come to redeem and restore his creation. Do you know what we call sent people? We call them _missionaries._

This is your new gospel identity as a follower of Jesus Christ. You are a _missionary._ You might think, _I am not a missionary. Missionaries take their families to remote areas of Africa to evangelize natives you might see in National Geographic—then you never hear from them again. That's a missionary. I'm not a missionary!_ However, if you look up "missionary" in the dictionary, it just means one sent on a mission. So where have we been sent? We are sent as missionaries to our family, neighborhood, workplace, schools, and every other sphere of life. In other words, we're given a mission to reach the people around us, wherever we are.

Some may question whether this truly applies to every follower of Jesus or only those sent to remote corners of the world—people who chose mission work as their full-time job. But Scripture answers this question without reservation.

> *Therefore, if anyone is in Christ, he is a new creation. The old has passed away; behold, the new has come. All this is from God, who through Christ reconciled us to himself and gave us the ministry of reconciliation; that is, in Christ God was reconciling the world to himself, not counting their trespasses against them, and entrusting to us the message of reconciliation. Therefore, we are ambassadors for Christ, God making his appeal through us. We implore you on behalf of Christ, be reconciled to God.*
>
> 2 Corinthians 5:17-21

We learn an important truth in this passage about sharing the gospel: everyone God saves, God sends. Just as Jesus explained that the disciples would be sent out in the same way he was, this text shows a similar parallel. Paul states that anyone who is in Jesus is reconciled to God through Christ's work, but that's not the end of the story. The result of our reconciliation is we are also entrusted with the mission to implore others to be reconciled to God. In our next study, we will look in more detail at this new activity which results from our new identity in Christ as missionaries.

Questions for Reflection

What cultural or religious baggage do you have attached to the word "missionary"? In what ways does that hinder you from living into this aspect of your identity in Christ?

_____

_____

_____

Where have you been sent? In what ways are you actively imploring others there to be reconciled to God?

_____

_____

_____

Do you believe that _everyone God saves, God sends?_ What excuses do we use to justify our unwillingness to live as missionaries?

_____

_____

_____

Prayer

Pray that God would use you right where you are to reconcile others to himself. Ask him to reveal those who need his salvation and to enable you to be his ambassador.

SCRIPTURE MEMORY

Therefore, _____ ambassadors for Christ, God _____ through us. We implore you on behalf of Christ, be _____ to God.

—2 Corinthians 5:20

OUR NEW PURPOSE

Scripture Study

2 CORINTHIANS 5:11-21

Therefore, knowing the fear of the Lord, we persuade others. But what we are is known to God, and I hope it is known also to your conscience. [12] We are not commending ourselves to you again but giving you cause to boast about us, so that you may be able to answer those who boast about outward appearance and not about what is in the heart. [13] For if we are beside ourselves, it is for God; if we are in our right mind, it is for you. [14] For the love of Christ controls us, because we have concluded this: that one has died for all, therefore all have died; [15] and he died for all, that those who live might no longer live for themselves but for him who for their sake died and was raised.

[16] From now on, therefore, we regard no one according to the flesh. Even though we once regarded Christ according to the flesh, we regard him thus no longer. [17] Therefore, if anyone is in Christ, he is a new creation. The old has passed away; behold, the new has come. [18] All this is from God, who through Christ reconciled us to himself and gave us the ministry of reconciliation; [19] that is, in Christ God was reconciling the world to himself, not counting their trespasses against them, and entrusting to us the message of reconciliation. [20] Therefore, we are ambassadors for Christ, God making

his appeal through us. We implore you on behalf of Christ, be reconciled to God. [21] For our sake he made him to be sin who knew no sin, so that in him we might become the righteousness of God.

Observing the Text

In verse 15, for whom does Paul say that we no longer live? And for whom then do we live?

_____

_____

_____

In verse 16, who does Paul now regard according to the flesh?

_____

_____

_____

For much of this passage, God is the one doing most of the action; what verb does Paul use to describe his own active role in verse 20?

_____

_____

_____

Interpreting the Text

What evidence do you see in verse 11 of identity (belief) leading to activity (behavior)? Do you see other instances of this throughout the passage?

_____

_____

_____

Why is it important that we no longer have the option to regard others according to the flesh? What does this look like?

_____

_____

_____

What are some synonyms for IMPLORE, as used by Paul in verse 20? In what ways does this word demonstrate Paul's intensity of purpose?

_____

_____

_____

Teaching

In the last lesson, we saw that our new gospel identity as missionaries beckons us to undertake the ministry of reconciliation. Before Jesus ascended to heaven, he gave more clarity to his followers on what this ministry of reconciliation would look like.

> Go therefore and make disciples of all nations, baptizing them in the name of the Father and of the Son and of the Holy Spirit, teaching them to observe all that I have commanded you. And behold, I am with you always, to the end of the age.
>
> Matthew 28:19-20

> But you will receive power when the Holy Spirit has come upon you, and you will be my witnesses in Jerusalem and in all Judea and Samaria, and to the end of the earth.
>
> Acts 1:8

How are we, as missionaries, to carry out the ministry of reconciliation? Jesus clearly said missionaries are to *go and multiply!* This is the gospel activity tied to our gospel identity as missionaries. Along with our new identity, we are given a new purpose in life: to participate in God's rescue mission by going into the world, declaring the gospel in word and demonstrating its power in deed in the hopes that followers of Jesus will be multiplied as a result.

This is gospel mission is sealed by the death and resurrection of Christ. Our clear calling is to reconcile others to God by sharing the good news of Jesus. We must not get shortsighted and redefine the Christian message with something a little more comfortable for us. We must not allow the mission of the local church to be diminished. Here are a few things to keep in mind:

- **The Church is not a self-improvement seminar.** When we see the church this way, we just want to use it to make our lives a little better—good kids and less stress, more comfort and happiness, pretty weddings and touching funerals—a little something to add meaning to our white-picket-fence world.

- **The Church is not a social service institution.** When we believe that the church's responsibility is simply to make the world a better place, we commit to good works—feeding the poor, practicing social justice, and being part of humanitarian aid efforts. These things are good and important, but if that's all we do then we fall short of God's plan for his people.

- **The Church is a rescue squad sent on a mission from God.** This is a mission that not only touches people's lives personally and influences our culture globally, but also impacts eternity. It is the only story that matters five minutes after we die and continues to matter a million years later. Everyone lives forever somewhere, and our ministry can impact another's eternity.

The Christian faith is a viral movement. You heard the message of the gospel from someone. They heard it from someone too. When the gospel came to you, it was on its way to someone else. Therefore, it must not stop with us. As missionaries, going and multiplying becomes our new purpose for living.

This isn't only important because of the potential impact on other people. When we don't live as missionaries, we are short-circuiting God's plan for our lives, choosing a lesser story that will not ultimately satisfy our hearts. God wrote eternity in our hearts. But we easily get intoxicated with smaller stories. The apostle Paul warns against this kind of distraction.

> *As for you, always be sober-minded, endure suffering, do the work of an evangelist, fulfill your ministry.*
>
> 2 Timothy 4:5

If you struggle to participate in God's mission, remember the teaching in the primer: work backwards through the gospel storyline.

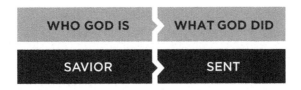

You are a *missionary*. If you don't see yourself with that gospel identity, go back to the fact that God sent you. If you don't see yourself as sent by God, go back to the gospel truth of *God as Savior.* When we see God as the Savior who, in Christ, rescued us from sin, we understand better that everyone that God saves and God sends. And if we are sent, that makes us missionaries. And if we are missionaries, then our new purpose in life is to go and multiply.

Questions for Reflection

In what ways do we redefine the message of Christ and diminish the mission of his church? How can your group fight against that temptation?

_____

_____

_____

Who shared the gospel with you? Who have you shared it with? How have you seen the viral spread of the gospel in your own experience?

_____

_____

_____

How well does your group reflect Paul's admonition to Timothy—sober-minded, enduring suffering, doing the work of evangelists, fulfilling your ministry? What can you do to help one another grow in this?

_____

_____

_____

Prayer

Thank God for including you in his plan to share his message of reconciliation to the world and pray that he would embolden you to join his mission as you go and multiply.

WEEKLY EXERCISE

REFLECTIONS ON BEING A MISSIONARY

Write out your thoughts and feelings about what it means to you having the gospel identity of a missionary. What implications do you believe this will have for your life? How do you see this identity tied to the gospel? Why is this important? Feel free to use another sheet of paper to better complete this exercise.

Get Ready for Group

Write your memorized Scripture.

_____

_____

_____

_____

_____

What observations and interpretations of Scripture were most meaningful to you?

_____

_____

_____

_____

_____

Summarize your key takeaway(s) for this week.

_____

_____

_____

_____

_____

What will you tell the group about the results of your exercise this week?

_____

_____

_____

_____

_____

How has this week helped you better understand and apply the Spiritual Growth Grid?

_____

_____

_____

_____

_____

	REPENT & BELIEVE		
WHO GOD IS	WHAT GOD DID	WHO WE ARE	WHAT WE DO
KING	CALLED	CITIZENS	LISTEN & OBEY
FATHER	ADOPTED	FAMILY	LOVE & SERVE
SAVIOR	SENT	MISSIONARIES	GO & MULTIPLY

03

FOUNDATIONS FOR MISSIONAL LIVING

SCRIPTURE MEMORY

But in your hearts honor Christ the Lord as holy, always being prepared to make a defense to anyone who asks you for a reason for the hope that is in you; yet do it with gentleness and respect...

—*1 Peter 3:15*

LIVING WITH CONFIDENCE

Scripture Study

JOHN 4:1-15

Now when Jesus learned that the Pharisees had heard that Jesus was making and baptizing more disciples than John ² (although Jesus himself did not baptize, but only his disciples), ³ he left Judea and departed again for Galilee. ⁴ And he had to pass through Samaria. ⁵ So he came to a town of Samaria called Sychar, near the field that Jacob had given to his son Joseph. ⁶ Jacob's well was there; so Jesus, wearied as he was from his journey, was sitting beside the well. It was about the sixth hour.

⁷ A woman from Samaria came to draw water. Jesus said to her, "Give me a drink." ⁸ (For his disciples had gone away into the city to buy food.) ⁹ The Samaritan woman said to him, "How is it that you, a Jew, ask for a drink from me, a woman of Samaria?" (For Jews have no dealings with Samaritans.) ¹⁰ Jesus answered her, "If you knew the gift of God, and who it is that is saying to you, 'Give me a drink,' you would have asked him, and he would have given you living water." ¹¹ The woman said to him, "Sir, you have nothing to draw water with, and the well is deep. Where do you get that living water?

[12] Are you greater than our father Jacob? He gave us the well and drank from it himself, as did his sons and his livestock." [13] Jesus said to her, "Everyone who drinks of this water will be thirsty again, [14] but whoever drinks of the water that I will give him will never be thirsty again. The water that I will give him will become in him a spring of water welling up to eternal life." [15] The woman said to him, "Sir, give me this water, so that I will not be thirsty or have to come here to draw water."

Observing the Text (verses 1-6)

Why did Jesus leave Judea?

_____

_____

_____

Where did Jesus go after leaving Judea?

_____

_____

_____

What time of the day was Jesus at the Jacob's well?

_____

_____

_____

Interpreting the Text (verses 1-6)

Why is Samaria such an important element to this story?

_____

_____

_____

What does this tell us about Jesus in that he was "wearied" from his journey?

_____

_____

_____

Why would Jesus go through a place like Samaria?

_____

_____

_____

Teaching

What obstacles are you allowing to hinder you from engaging the world? We can all come up with a dozen reasons why we can't talk to our parents, neighbor, co-worker, or friend about the gospel. But, we must fight against making excuses because the mission is too important. The love of God displayed in Christ is too marvelous to allow anything to get in the way of proclaiming it. Like Jesus, we must not allow any obstacle to hinder us from engaging others.

Jesus lived with complete confidence, clearly seen in John 4 as he interacted with the woman from Samaria. He wasn't arrogant, because his confidence was placed in something beyond mere human ability. As followers of Jesus, we can imitate him by placing our confidence in the same two objects that he trusted in.

First, we must have confidence in God. Jesus knew himself and the Father. He neither had to be reminded of his own power, majesty, holiness, and greatness nor of God the Father's qualities and worth. No matter who stood before him—king, slave, rich, poor, or a troubled Samaritan woman—Jesus wasn't intimidated. He knew that God, and his plan for the world, were both perfect and complete.

We see this confidence in John 4:10 when the woman wonders why Jesus is asking her for a drink. Jesus responds with this incredible statement: "If you knew the gift of God, and who it is that is saying to you, 'Give me a drink,' you would have asked him, and he would have given you living water." He is confident in who he is, and we should be confident in who he is as well. We should trust that God is the very center of power, love, and grace. He is the answer.

Second, we must have confidence in the gospel message. Jesus knows he is the only hope for every man, woman, and child. We see this confidence in verses 13-14:

> Jesus said to her, "Everyone who drinks of this water will be thirsty again, but whoever drinks of the water that I will give him will never be thirsty again. The water that I will give him will become in him a spring of water welling up to eternal life."

Although the woman's need was overwhelming, Jesus didn't hesitate or waver. He was never overwhelmed by anyone's sin. On the contrary, sin was overwhelmed by him. That's why Jesus never encountered a life that was too far gone from him to rescue. He knew who he was and what he was going to do at the cross. He knew he had come to bring new life!

The Church today suffers from a confidence problem. Our culture may seem to be growing more hostile to Jesus and his gospel message, but that does not change God or his plan to redeem the world. Are you someone who has complete confidence that God's message of hope in Christ is the right message? Are you convinced, like Jesus, no matter who is in front of you—no matter how strong, intelligent, sinful, hardhearted, or far gone they seem—that "the gospel is the power of God unto salvation for all who believe" (Romans 1:16)? This confidence is foundational for living effectively as a missionary.

Intimidation can arise when our eyes become fixed on the person we are sharing with instead of on Jesus. This is not to suggest looking past or trivializing people, but to fix our eyes upon Jesus, never losing sight of who he is and the power of the gospel he brings. To fail to do so risks becoming easily overwhelmed by shifting our focus to the problems, questions, or intellect of the people we're trying to reach. Confidence shrinks as well as our desire to share the gospel.

Do you believe God is wonderful and glorious? Do you believe in his message of reconciliation? Are you convinced the gospel is the hope for every man, woman, and child? Be confident in God and the gospel he offers!

Questions for Reflection

What obstacles are you allowing to hinder you from engaging the world? What excuses and rationalizations do you employ to justify your inactivity on behalf of the gospel?

_____

_____

_____

Why is it difficult to share the gospel when we place our confidence in ourselves and our abilities?

_____

_____

_____

How can your group help each other to fix your eyes on God and his gospel, placing your confidence in him and allowing this to transform your interactions with those you're trying to reach?

_____

_____

_____

Prayer

Pray by name for someone on your Top 5 that God would use your words and actions to show them the beauty of Christ and his gospel. Thank him for being worthy of our confidence and ask him to strengthen your faith in Him and the sufficiency of the message.

SCRIPTURE MEMORY

But in your _____ honor Christ the
Lord as holy, always being prepared
to make a defense to anyone who asks
you for a reason for the hope that is
in you; yet do it with _____ and
respect...

—1 Peter 3:15

COMPELLED BY LOVE

Scripture Study

JOHN 4:1-15

Now when Jesus learned that the Pharisees had heard that Jesus was making and baptizing more disciples than John [2] *(although Jesus himself did not baptize, but only his disciples),* [3] *he left Judea and departed again for Galilee.* [4] *And he had to pass through Samaria.* [5] *So he came to a town of Samaria called Sychar, near the field that Jacob had given to his son Joseph.* [6] *Jacob's well was there; so Jesus, wearied as he was from his journey, was sitting beside the well. It was about the sixth hour.*

[7] *A woman from Samaria came to draw water. Jesus said to her, "Give me a drink."* [8] *(For his disciples had gone away into the city to buy food.)* [9] *The Samaritan woman said to him, "How is it that you, a Jew, ask for a drink from me, a woman of Samaria?" (For Jews have no dealings with Samaritans.)* [10] *Jesus answered her, "If you knew the gift of God, and who it is that is saying to you, 'Give me a drink,' you would have asked him, and he would have given you living water."* [11] *The woman said to him, "Sir, you have nothing to draw water with, and the well is deep. Where do you get that living water?* [12] *Are you greater than our father Jacob? He gave us the well and drank from it himself, as did his sons and his livestock."* [13] *Jesus said to her, "Everyone*

67

who drinks of this water will be thirsty again, [14] but whoever drinks of the water that I will give him will never be thirsty again. The water that I will give him will become in him a spring of water welling up to eternal life." [15] The woman said to him, "Sir, give me this water, so that I will not be thirsty or have to come here to draw water."

Observing the text (verses 7-15)

What did Jesus ask for the Samaritan woman to give him?

_____

_____

What was her response to Jesus?

_____

_____

_____

Interpreting the text (verses 7-15)

Why do you think Jesus initiated a conversation with this Samaritan woman?

_____

_____

_____

How would you characterize the woman's response to Jesus?

_____

_____

_____

Teaching

It is sad that the American church is better known for what we are *against* rather than who and what we are *for*. To be fair, we are not entirely to blame. There are spiritual forces at work which hate us and would continue to do so even if we did everything correctly. Jesus reminds us in John 15:18, "If the world hates you, know that it has hated me before it hated you." However, no matter how much hate we endure, as God's people we need to hold fast to what drives our gospel mission: love. It's an essential part of the foundation for missional living.

The gospel message cannot be divorced from love. Our engagement with lost people should find its roots in our love for God and his glory. It was the great desire of Jesus to see his Father glorified above all else (John 17:1-5). Everything Jesus did was done to show his love for the Father (John 14:31). In Matthew 22:37, when asked what the greatest commandment of the Scripture was, Jesus answered, "You shall love the Lord your God with all your heart and with all your soul and with all your mind." Do you have a genuine love for God that fuels your life? If the people you spend the most time with were asked to describe you, would the first thing out of their mouth be your love for God? We must seek to be driven by love for God in the mission of making disciples. Evangelism was never meant to be a spiritual drudgery we slavishly perform but a glorious calling fueled by an ever-deepening love and awe for the one who first loved us.

If we grow in loving God, we will then be moved to love the lost as well. It's no coincidence that Jesus followed his statement about loving God with these words, calling them the second greatest commandment: "You shall love your neighbor as yourself" (Matthew 22:39). This was the reason Jesus was called the friend of sinners. He loved others well—all kinds of others, especially those that everyone else wrote off as too broken, dirty, or evil. We must love others as Christ loved them in order to fulfill our new mission in life.

So, what motivated Jesus to speak with the woman at the well? Not only was it love for his Father but also for the woman herself. There was a reason she went alone to retrieve water at the sixth hour (around noon). Women usually went in groups earlier in the day, but this woman was an outcast because of sinful choices she made that put her on the fringes of society. Every day she would walk to the well and be reminded of her shame. This is probably why she asked Jesus for living water so she would not be thirsty and have to come back to the well. Yet Jesus treats her with compassion even when he names her sin. If we could speak with this woman, or the untouchable leper in Mark 2, or hated tax collector Zacchaeus in Luke 19, they would all without a doubt say Jesus loved them well.

Do you have a genuine love for people? Do you love, not just for the ones who are easy to love, but, as Jesus modeled, those who are difficult? Would the people around you say you love them well? May we, as missionaries, be people who are compelled by love!

Questions for Reflection
If the people you spend the most time with were asked to describe you, would the first thing out of their mouth be your love for God? Why or why not?

_____

_____

_____

Would the people around you say you love them well?

_____

_____

_____

In what ways do you struggle to love others? Why is it sometimes difficult to move from loving others to sharing Christ with them?

_____

_____

_____

Prayer

Praise God for his gracious, unbelievable love extended to you, even while you were still in the depths of your sin. Pray that he would help you to see others as he does – lost children in need of grace and truth – and to love them with his perfect love.

SCRIPTURE MEMORY

But in your hearts _____ Christ the Lord as ____, always being prepared to make a _____ to anyone who asks you for a reason for the hope that is __ you; yet do it with gentleness and respect...

—*1 Peter 3:15*

STRIVING TO BE INTENTIONAL

Scripture Study

JOHN 4:1-15

Now when Jesus learned that the Pharisees had heard that Jesus was making and baptizing more disciples than John [2] *(although Jesus himself did not baptize, but only his disciples),* [3] *he left Judea and departed again for Galilee.* [4] *And he had to pass through Samaria.* [5] *So he came to a town of Samaria called Sychar, near the field that Jacob had given to his son Joseph.* [6] *Jacob's well was there; so Jesus, wearied as he was from his journey, was sitting beside the well. It was about the sixth hour.*

[7] *A woman from Samaria came to draw water. Jesus said to her, "Give me a drink."* [8] *(For his disciples had gone away into the city to buy food.)* [9] *The Samaritan woman said to him, "How is it that you, a Jew, ask for a drink from me, a woman of Samaria?" (For Jews have no dealings with Samaritans.)* [10] *Jesus answered her, "If you knew the gift of God, and who it is that is saying to you, 'Give me a drink,' you would have asked him, and he would have given you living water."* [11] *The woman said to him, "Sir, you have nothing to draw water with, and the well is deep. Where do you get that living water?*

[12] *Are you greater than our father Jacob? He gave us the well and drank from it himself, as did his sons and his livestock."* [13] *Jesus said to her, "Everyone who drinks of this water will be thirsty again,* [14] *but whoever drinks of the water that I will give him will never be thirsty again. The water that I will give him will become in him a spring of water welling up to eternal life."* [15] *The woman said to him, "Sir, give me this water, so that I will not be thirsty or have to come here to draw water."*

Observing the Text (verses 7-15)

What kind of water did Jesus say that he could give to the woman?

_____

_____

_____

How does Jesus describe this "living water"?

_____

_____

_____

What claim did Jesus make about the result of drinking the water he gives?

_____

_____

_____

Interpreting the Text (verses 7-15)

How does the woman's reference to Jacob highlight Jesus' authority?

_____

_____

_____

What does Jesus mean by "living water" in this passage?

_____

_____

_____

Teaching

Missionaries sent by their Savior to go and multiply must be intentional. Missionaries are called to live with intentionality in four areas.

First, missionaries live with intentionality in their pursuit of God. The gospel writers highlight several times how Jesus spent intentional time with the Father in prayer. The great gift of the gospel is that we have been given access to God (Ephesians 2:18). We must pursue an ever-deepening relationship with God through his Word as one of our highest values. John 15 tells us that apart from God's work in us, we can do nothing of spiritual consequence. We must intentionally pursue God.

Second, missionaries live with intentionality in their relationships. Because Jesus loves his Father, it brought him great joy to reveal him to others. The same should be true of us. Jesus was very intentional with every relationship he had. Some of us have lived next to neighbors for years and have barely spoken to them, let alone shared the gospel. The same can be said of co-workers, friends, and family. We must be intentional as missionaries with the relationships God gives us. What relationships has God given you to this end?

Third, missionaries live with intentionality in every opportunity. It would have been very easy for Jesus to not speak with the Samaritan woman in John 4. When she showed up at the well, Jesus could have gotten up and walked somewhere else. He could have simply ignored her. But he didn't. Instead, he made the most of the opportunity. So many of us go through life needing to accomplish our tasks and viewing people as obstacles in our way. But what if we looked at things differently? What if we looked at the tasks we have to accomplish—going to work, getting groceries, buying gas, eating out, going to the gym, volunteering at our children's school, etc.—as opportunities to engage people? Missionaries value intentionality at every opportunity.

Finally, missionaries live with intentionality in the places they go and the things that they do. John 4:4 says Jesus intentionally went through Samaria, "And he had to pass through Samaria." Jesus would have been applauded and encouraged by the religious leaders of his day to avoid going to Samaria (the Jews detested Samaritans during this time). Why did he *have* to go? Could it have been to speak to this woman who he would use to bring salvation to an entire village? Jesus had the Father's mission in mind, even while making his itinerary.

Christians are good at huddling together. We have Christian sports leagues, dance studios, book stores, music, comedians, movies, and even our own breath mints! These things are not wrong in and of themselves (except for Christian breath mints—always a bad idea), but they can also be tremendous roadblocks to reaching the world around us. They can devolve into holy huddles and spiritual cul-de-sacs which fight against going and multiplying. If we are not careful, they can foster anti-missional attitudes in believers.

But missionaries learn from Christ by imitating his intentionality as they position themselves to interact with the lost world around them. They are intentional at the ballpark, schoolyard, workplace, restaurant, golf course, and anywhere else they find themselves. Missionaries even ask where there is no gospel presence and seek to go there as well. Where can they go where Christians usually don't? Intentionality is key.

In sum, the foundation for living a missional life is having confidence in God and his gospel, being compelled by love, and seeking intentionality. These are qualities of missionaries who effectively go and multiply.

Questions for Reflection

Are you intentionally pursuing your relationship with God? Why is this foundational to the life of a missionary?

_____

_____

_____

In what areas do you struggle with prioritizing tasks over people? In what opportunities do you need to be more intentional?

_____

_____

_____

What are the various positives and negatives of organizations or settings that are exclusively Christian? How have your opportunities for missional living been affected?

_____

_____

_____

Prayer

Thank God for his intentionality in leading you to Jesus and pray that he would "lift up your eyes" to see the opportunities to engage those around you in gospel relationships.

WEEKLY EXERCISE

———

SPHERES OF INFLUENCE & TOP 5

This activity will help you identify your circles of accountability, also known as our Spheres of Influence. Take note of the non-believers with whom you can build intentional relationships. Get to know them, pray for them, serve them, and find opportunities to share your grace story and the gospel

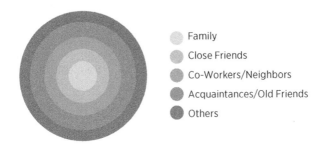

Family
Close Friends
Co-Workers/Neighbors
Acquaintances/Old Friends
Others

FAMILY

NON-BELIEVERS   BELIEVERS

_____   _____

_____   _____

_____   _____

_____   _____

CLOSE FRIENDS

NON-BELIEVERS   BELIEVERS

_____   _____

_____   _____

_____   _____

_____   _____

CO-WORKERS/NEIGHBORS

NON-BELIEVERS   BELIEVERS

_____   _____

_____   _____

_____   _____

_____   _____

AQUAINTANCES/OLD FRIENDS

NON-BELIEVERS   BELIEVERS

_____   _____

_____   _____

_____   _____

_____   _____

OTHERS

NON-BELIEVERS   BELIEVERS

_____   _____

_____   _____

_____   _____

_____   _____

Of these relationships with non-believers, choose the five biggest priorities for prayer. This is your Top 5:

1. _____   4. _____

2. _____   5. _____

3. _____

Get Ready for Group

Write your memorized Scripture.

_____

_____

_____

_____

_____

What observations and interpretations of Scripture were most meaningful
to you?

_____

_____

_____

_____

Summarize your key takeaway(s) for this week.

_____

_____

_____

_____

_____

What will you tell the group about the results of your exercise this week?

_____

_____

_____

_____

How has this week helped you better understand and apply the Spiritual Growth Grid?

_____

_____

_____

_____

_____

		REPENT & BELIEVE	
WHO GOD IS	WHAT GOD DID	WHO WE ARE	WHAT WE DO
KING	CALLED	CITIZENS	LISTEN & OBEY
FATHER	ADOPTED	FAMILY	LOVE & SERVE
SAVIOR	SENT	MISSIONARIES	GO & MULTIPLY

04

MISSIONAL PRAYER

SCRIPTURE MEMORY

But in your hearts honor Christ the Lord as holy, always being prepared to make a defense to anyone who asks you for a reason for the hope that is in you; yet do it with gentleness and respect...

—*1 Peter 3:15*

BEGIN WITH PRAYER

Scripture Study

JOHN 4:16-42

Jesus said to her, "Go, call your husband, and come here." ⁷ The woman answered him, "I have no husband." Jesus said to her, "You are right in saying, 'I have no husband'; ¹⁸ *for you have had five husbands, and the one you now have is not your husband. What you have said is true." ¹⁹ The woman said to him, "Sir, I perceive that you are a prophet. ²⁰ Our fathers worshiped on this mountain, but you say that in Jerusalem is the place where people ought to worship." ²¹ Jesus said to her, "Woman, believe me, the hour is coming when neither on this mountain nor in Jerusalem will you worship the Father.* ²² *You worship what you do not know; we worship what we know, for salvation is from the Jews. ²³ But the hour is coming, and is now here, when the true worshipers will worship the Father in spirit and truth, for the Father is seeking such people to worship him. ²⁴ God is spirit, and those who worship him must worship in spirit and truth." ²⁵ The woman said to him, "I know that Messiah is coming (he who is called Christ). When he comes, he will tell us all things." ²⁶ Jesus said to her, "I who speak to you am he."*

²⁷ *Just then his disciples came back. They marveled that he was talking with a woman, but no one said, "What do you seek?" or, "Why are you talking*

with her?" [28] So the woman left her water jar and went away into town and said to the people, [29] "Come, see a man who told me all that I ever did. Can this be the Christ?" [30] They went out of the town and were coming to him.

[31] Meanwhile the disciples were urging him, saying, "Rabbi, eat." [32] But he said to them, "I have food to eat that you do not know about." [33] So the disciples said to one another, "Has anyone brought him something to eat?" [34] Jesus said to them, "My food is to do the will of him who sent me and to accomplish his work. [35] Do you not say, 'There are yet four months, then comes the harvest'? Look, I tell you, lift up your eyes, and see that the fields are white for harvest. [36] Already the one who reaps is receiving wages and gathering fruit for eternal life, so that sower and reaper may rejoice together. [37] For here the saying holds true, 'One sows and another reaps.' [38] I sent you to reap that for which you did not labor. Others have labored, and you have entered into their labor."

[39] Many Samaritans from that town believed in him because of the woman's testimony, "He told me all that I ever did." [40] So when the Samaritans came to him, they asked him to stay with them, and he stayed there two days. [41] And many more believed because of his word. [42] They said to the woman, "It is no longer because of what you said that we believe, for we have heard for ourselves, and we know that this is indeed the Savior of the world.

Observing the Text (verses 16-20)

Who does Jesus tell the woman to go and get?

_____

_____

_____

How does Jesus reply to the woman's response to his question?

_____

_____

What is the woman's observation about Jesus?

_____

_____

_____

Interpreting the Text (verses 16-20)

Why do you think that Jesus brings up the woman's marriage situation?

_____

_____

_____

Why does she bring up a question about the right place to worship?

_____

_____

_____

What reasons would cause the woman not divert the conversation about her five marriages?

_____

_____

_____

Teaching

In this study so far we have clearly defined the gospel and learned how it gives us our identity as missionaries who are sent into the world to go and multiply. We have discussed how important it is to lay a missional foundation composed of confidence, love, and intentionality. We have also begun an activity which helps followers of Jesus define their "mission field" by identifying your Spheres of Influence.

The next few weeks will be given to answering the question of how we should begin to impact the lives of the people Jesus sent us to reach. Asked another way, *how do missionaries have a gospel presence in the world around them?* A simple way to remember what we do as missionaries is the acrostic BLESS[1]. It stands for:

- Begin with prayer
- Listen and be aware of the needs of those in your spheres of influence
- Eat with your lost neighbors, co-workers, and friends
- Serve—find ways to engage those in your spheres with good deeds that might open a door for the good news
- Share* the gospel—tell your grace story and declare the goodness of God

Notice that sharing the word of the gospel with those within our Spheres of Influence comes after intentionally engaging them by deed. This is why missionaries are those who engage their world for the gospel by word and deed.

The first step of BLESS will be this week's focus: Begin with prayer. We must not dismiss this important element. Who should you pray for as a missionary? What does missional prayer include? Once again, this is why we've developed our Spheres of Influence.

Praying for those in our Spheres of Influence heightens our awareness of our missional interactions in their lives. Not only do we bring requests to God on behalf of our friends but praying for them serves as a heart "checkup" for us. The more we pray for those in our Spheres of Influence, the more we become cognizant of how we are or aren't intentionally making inroads in their lives for the gospel. Questions like "When was

---

1 Adapted from Dave Ferguson, "Five Ways to Bless Your Neighbors," www.vergenetwork. org/2012/12/27/five-ways-to-bless-your-neighbors-dave-ferguson, accessed 10-25-2016.

the last time we shared a meal?" "Do I have time to call them soon?"or "How am I strategically investing my life in theirs?" can easily surface in our thoughts after we spend regular time praying for our lost friends and neighbors.

This kind of praying is called *intercession.* It is simply followers of Jesus praying for others. 1 Timothy 2:1 says, "First of all, then, I urge that supplications, prayers, intercessions, and thanksgivings be made for all people." A missionary realizes praying for "all people" includes those in his or her Spheres of Influence.

God has called his people to intercede for others because ultimately he has ordained to work through the prayers of his people. That's the chief reason we pray and the main reason the Bible calls us to it. God has chosen to work through your prayers on behalf of others. Can God do his will without our prayers? Absolutely! But praying allows us to join him in his work. This is especially important to know when it comes to salvation, and why the first action of BLESS is to begin with prayer. Missionaries who seek to impact the lost around them for the gospel begin with prayer.

Questions for Reflection

Who do you need to be praying for in your Sphere of Influence? What keeps you from doing so?

_____

_____

_____

In what way does intercession impact your affections for and actions toward others?

_____

_____

_____

How has a lack of prayer for others revealed a struggle to believe that you have been sent as a missionary? In what ways do you need to repent and grow in faith?

_____

_____

_____

Prayer

Pray for those within your Sphere of Influence – that they would see God's goodness and embrace the good news. Ask God to provide opportunities for you to engage them with truth and love.

SCRIPTURE MEMORY

But in your hearts honor Christ the Lord as holy, always being prepared to make a _____ to anyone who asks you for a reason for the _____ _____; yet do it with gentleness and respect...

—1 Peter 3:15

PRAYING FOR GOD TO MOVE

Scripture Study

JOHN 4:16-42

Jesus said to her, "Go, call your husband, and come here." 17 The woman answer him, "I have no husband." Jesus said to her, "You are right in saying, 'I have no husband'; 18 for you have had five husbands, and the one you now have is not your husband. What you have said is true." 19 The woman said to him, "Sir, I perceive that you are a prophet. 20 Our fathers worshiped on this mountain, but you say that in Jerusalem is the place where people ought to worship." 21 Jesus said to her, "Woman, believe me, the hour is coming when neither on this mountain nor in Jerusalem will you worship the Father. 22 You worship what you do not know; we worship what we know, for salvation is from the Jews. 23 But the hour is coming, and is now here, when the true worshipers will worship the Father in spirit and truth, for the Father is seeking such people to worship him. 24 God is spirit, and those who worship him must worship in spirit and truth." 25 The woman said to him, "I know that Messiah is coming (he who is called Christ). When he comes, he will tell us all things." 26 Jesus said to her, "I who speak to you am he."

[27] *Just then his disciples came back. They marveled that he was talking with a woman, but no one said, "What do you seek?" or, "Why are you talking with her?" [28] So the woman left her water jar and went away into town and said to the people, [29] "Come, see a man who told me all that I ever did. Can this be the Christ?" [30] They went out of the town and were coming to him.*

[31] Meanwhile the disciples were urging him, saying, "Rabbi, eat." [32] But he said to them, "I have food to eat that you do not know about." [33] So the disciples said to one another, "Has anyone brought him something to eat?" [34] Jesus said to them, "My food is to do the will of him who sent me and to accomplish his work. [35] Do you not say, 'There are yet four months, then comes the harvest'? Look, I tell you, lift up your eyes, and see that the fields are white for harvest. [36] Already the one who reaps is receiving wages and gathering fruit for eternal life, so that sower and reaper may rejoice together. [37] For here the saying holds true, 'One sows and another reaps.' [38] I sent you to reap that for which you did not labor. Others have labored, and you have entered into their labor."

[39] Many Samaritans from that town believed in him because of the woman's testimony, "He told me all that I ever did." [40] So when the Samaritans came to him, they asked him to stay with them, and he stayed there two days. [41] And many more believed because of his word. [42] They said to the woman, "It is no longer because of what you said that we believe, for we have heard for ourselves, and we know that this is indeed the Savior of the world.

Observing the text (verses 21-26)

What does Jesus say is so special about the season both he and the woman are about to enter?

_____

_____

_____

What kind of worshippers is the Father seeking?

_____

_____

_____

In verse 26, who does Jesus claim to be?

_____

_____

_____

Interpreting the text (verses 21-16)

Why do you think that Jesus brings up the woman's marriage situation?

_____

_____

_____

What does Jesus mean when he says that "salvation is from the Jews"?

_____

_____

_____

What does it look like to "worship in spirit and truth"?

_____

_____

_____

Teaching

There are times in the Scripture when we're given a look behind the scenes into how God secretly operates. Often, we don't see this reality, only notic-ing what's in front of our eyes. But here and there the Bible records not only what is seen but also what is unseen and gives us a sense of what's really happening.

In Acts 16 we have the conversion account of a woman named Lydia. Based on what we read in many stories in the New Testament, we might expect the Bible to simply say, "And Lydia believed." But there's more; we actually get to see how God is working behind the scenes.

Before we read, let's understand the context. Paul and his church-plant-ing team are making their way to the town of Philippi, where the usual strategy would begin with finding a synagogue where the apostle could speak to his fellow Jews about Jesus the Messiah. But, Philippi has such a small Jewish presence that they can't find a synagogue to attend on the Sabbath. They hear about a place outside the town where Jewish women gather to pray, so Paul and his team find them in order to share the gospel with them. Listen to how Acts 16:13-15 describes the account:

> And on the Sabbath day we went outside the gate to the river-side, where we supposed there was a place of prayer, and we sat down and spoke to the women who had come together. One who heard us was a woman named Lydia, from the city of Thyatira, a seller of purple goods, who was a worshiper of God. **The Lord opened her heart to pay attention** to what was said by Paul. And after she was baptized, and her household as well, she urged us, saying, "If you have judged me to be faithful to the Lord, come to my house and stay." And she prevailed upon us.

Did you catch that? Paul shares the message about Jesus and instead of simply telling us "Lydia believed," the curtain is pulled back for us, revealing the inner workings of God.

God enabled Lydia to not only understand the message about Jesus but to believe it for herself. She was changed. Lydia became a follower of Jesus! That's why the very next verse speaks of her baptism and that of her household as well.

This is important for missionaries because it tells us what must take place in order for us to multiply as we go. God must first work in the hearts of the lost in order for them to believe. Our response to this truth is clear: we must talk to God about our friends before we talk to our friends about God.

Why would God do salvation this way? Why does it take his divine initiative to believe? It seems like people should be able to find and believe God on their own. Let's look at what the Bible says about each of us before we believe in Christ:

> In their case the god of this world has blinded the minds of the unbelievers, to keep them from seeing the light of the gospel of the glory of Christ, who is the image of God.
>
> 2 Corinthians 4:4

That's pretty clear. Unbelievers are spiritually blinded by Satan so that they would be kept "from seeing the light of the gospel of the glory of Christ." Put another way, our hearts, by default, are closed to the gospel. Sure, we can read about it, hear about it, and talk about it, but Satan leverages our brokenness against us so that the gospel never becomes so essential, beautiful, and treasured that we'd give anything and everything for it.

However, it's not only Satan that is a roadblock to finding Christ on our own; we also start off spiritually ruined from square one. When Adam and Eve sinned in the Garden of Eden, they brought corruption to all of humanity. Thus, while we are born physically alive, we are spiritually dead. Paul confirms this in his letter to the Ephesians: "And you were dead in the trespasses and sins...and were by nature children of wrath, like the rest of mankind" (Ephesians 2:1, 3). We're so dead, so spiritually incapacitated, that we don't seek God nor can we perform well enough to merit his salvation. Romans 3:10b-12 says, "None is righteous, no, not one; no one understands; no one seeks for God. All have turned aside; together they have become worthless; no one does good, not even one."

God must take the initiative in salvation. If he doesn't move, we never will. As sinners we're too broken, enslaved, and incapacitated. That's why missionaries begin with prayer before anything else. They ask God to move first, opening hearts and minds to the truth about Jesus. They regularly lift in prayer those in their Spheres of Influence. Missionaries know they must talk to God about their friends before they talk to their friends about God. They consistently ask God to bring about what only he can.

Questions for Reflection

Describe a time when you have seen God work within someone in a way that they would not have been capable of on their own.

_____

_____

_____

In what ways is it countercultural to believe that unbelievers are spiritually blinded until God works within them? Why can it be a struggle to believe that God must take the initiative in salvation?

_____

_____

_____

Do you make it a priority to talk to God about your Top 5 before you talk to your Top 5 about God? Why or why not?

_____

_____

_____

Prayer

Pray that God would begin to draw your Top 5 to himself and open their hearts to his gospel. Ask him to give them a desire for Christ and to give you an opportunity to share.

SCRIPTURE MEMORY

But in your hearts _____ the

Lord as holy, always being prepared

to make a defense to anyone who asks

you for a reason for the hope that is

in you; yet do it with _____

_____

—1 Peter 3:15

WHAT TO PRAY FOR

Scripture Study

JOHN 4:16-42

Jesus said to her, "Go, call your husband, and come here." [17] The woman answered him, "I have no husband." Jesus said to her, "You are right in saying, 'I have no husband'; [18] for you have had five husbands, and the one you now have is not your husband. What you have said is true." [19] The woman said to him, "Sir, I perceive that you are a prophet. [20] Our fathers worshiped on this mountain, but you say that in Jerusalem is the place where people ought to worship." [21] Jesus said to her, "Woman, believe me, the hour is coming when neither on this mountain nor in Jerusalem will you worship the Father. [22] You worship what you do not know; we worship what we know, for salvation is from the Jews. [23] But the hour is coming, and is now here, when the true worshipers will worship the Father in spirit and truth, for the Father is seeking such people to worship him. [24] God is spirit, and those who worship him must worship in spirit and truth." [25] The woman said to him, "I know that Messiah is coming (he who is called Christ). When he comes, he will tell us all things." [26] Jesus said to her, "I who speak to you am he."

[27] Just then his disciples came back. They marveled that he was talking with a woman, but no one said, "What do you seek?" or, "Why are you talking

with her?" [28] So the woman left her water jar and went away into town and said to the people, [29] "Come, see a man who told me all that I ever did. Can this be the Christ?" [30] They went out of the town and were coming to him.

[31] Meanwhile the disciples were urging him, saying, "Rabbi, eat." [32] But he said to them, "I have food to eat that you do not know about." [33] So the disciples said to one another, "Has anyone brought him something to eat?" [34] Jesus said to them, "My food is to do the will of him who sent me and to accomplish his work. [35] Do you not say, 'There are yet four months, then comes the harvest'? Look, I tell you, lift up your eyes, and see that the fields are white for harvest. [36] Already the one who reaps is receiving wages and gathering fruit for eternal life, so that sower and reaper may rejoice together. [37] For here the saying holds true, 'One sows and another reaps.' [38] I sent you to reap that for which you did not labor. Others have labored, and you have entered into their labor."

[39] Many Samaritans from that town believed in him because of the woman's testimony, "He told me all that I ever did." [40] So when the Samaritans came to him, they asked him to stay with them, and he stayed there two days. [41] And many more believed because of his word. [42] They said to the woman, "It is no longer because of what you said that we believe, for we have heard for ourselves, and we know that this is indeed the Savior of the world.

Observing the Text (verses 27-42)

How did the woman respond to Jesus' claim to be the Messiah?

_____

_____

_____

What does Jesus say is his food?

_____

_____

How did the people of the town respond to the woman's story?

_____

_____

_____

Interpreting the Text (verses 27-42)

Describe the difference of purpose between Jesus and his disciples in this passage.

_____

_____

_____

What did Jesus mean when he said, "My food is to do the will of him who sent me and to accomplish his work" in verse 34?

_____

_____

_____

Why did the Samaritans initially believe? How did their belief change by the end of the passage?

_____

_____

_____

Teaching

As we've examined this week, prayer for the lost is essential in the life of a missionary. It's why the BLESS acrostic begins with us seeking God on behalf of those in our Spheres of Influence. We need God to take the initiative in salvation. The followers of Jesus in the early church knew this to be true.

- In 2 Timothy 2:25-26, Paul tells his protégé, Timothy, to deal with his detractors in such a way that, "**God may perhaps grant them** repentance leading to a knowledge of the truth, and they may come to their senses and escape from the snare of the devil, after being captured by him to do his will."

- In Acts 11:18, when church leaders saw Gentiles believing the gospel, they concluded the same thing, "When they heard these things they fell silent. And they glorified God, saying, 'Then to the Gentiles also **God has granted** repentance that leads to life.'"

- When speaking to the Christians of Philippi in Philippians 1:29, Paul says, "For **it has been granted** to you that for the sake of Christ you should...believe in him."

This is why the leaders of the early church, wanting to see people believe the gospel, naturally turned to prayer. They sought God's saving intervention in the lives of those they were trying to reach.

This is also why we talk about our Top 5, the list of five individuals we personally and regularly pray to come to faith in Christ. Here are four specific things that you can pray for those on your Top 5 list:

An opportunity to share the gospel
Don't take the easy road of praying for a friend's salvation but avoiding your potential role in it. Ask God to use you in the lives of those in your Spheres of Influence. Pray to be an instrument of God's grace to your friend. Look to Paul's example in Colossians 4:3-4:

At the same time, pray also for us, that God may open to us a door for the word, to declare the mystery of Christ, on account of which I am in prison—that I may make it clear, which is how I ought to speak.

Notice this request rests on the foundation that God must first move. He has to open a door of opportunity, leading us to our next specific prayer.

Boldness to take advantage of that opportunity

Paul says to the church in Ephesians 6:18b-20:

> *To that end keep alert with all perseverance, making supplication for all the saints, and also for me, that **words may be given to me in opening my mouth boldly to proclaim** the mystery of the gospel, for which I am an ambassador in chains, **that I may declare it boldly, as I ought to speak.***

This can be scary. No one wants to feel rejected or ridiculed. So we pray for confidence that God is at work and wants to use us as instruments to bring our friends to Jesus.

Receptivity to the gospel

Pray that those within our Spheres of Influence would honor the word we give by receiving it into their hearts. 2 Thessalonians 3:1 says, "Finally, brothers, pray for us, *that the word of the Lord may speed ahead and be honored,* as happened among you..." One could pray, "God, I need you to do what I can't—to open their eyes, give them a new heart, and move them to treasure Jesus for who he is and what he's done."

Finally, we can also pray that God would bring other believers into the lives of those on our Top 5 list. Since all of Christ's people are his missionaries, we should want as many Christians as possible in the lives of these people. God has tethered himself to his Church, and the gospel becomes accessible through their lives as they are present with those who do not believe.

We're reminded of Acts 14:27, when Paul reported on his first missionary journey: "And when they arrived and gathered the church together, they declared all that God had done with them, and how he *had opened a door of faith to the Gentiles.*" We can pray, "God, open a door of faith for them. Use me. Use others. Someway, somehow, I pray that you would bring them to yourself."

Jesus knew God's initiative in the life of the lost is the only hope any of us have. Christ said in John 6:44, "No one can come to me unless the Father who sent me draws him." He knew God must move first. This is why, as missionaries who've been sent by God with a new purpose, prayer is where we begin (remember, think BLESS). May we commit to developing a life of missional prayer.

Questions for Reflection

Why is it important to pray not only for the salvation of our Top 5, but also for an opportunity for us to be involved? Which is easier for you, the praying or the sharing?

_____

_____

_____

How often do you pray for boldness in your relationships? Do we sometimes see this as a personality trait rather than an area of obedience?

_____

_____

_____

What other believers are present in the lives of your Top 5? How can you encourage and support those relationships?

_____

_____

_____

Prayer

Thank God for allowing you to be his instrument in the lives of your Top 5 and pray that he would give you opportunities to boldly share with those whose hearts he has made receptive to his gospel.

WEEKLY
EXERCISE

———

LIVING WITH INTENTIONALITY

Write down the activities you are a part of each week. This will help you identify specific activities you are a part of to begin living with intentionality as a gospel presence.

MONDAY   TUESDAY   WEDNESDAY

_____   _____   _____

_____   _____   _____

_____   _____   _____

THURSDAY   FRIDAY   SATURDAY

_____   _____   _____

_____   _____   _____

_____   _____   _____

SUNDAY   MONTHLY/OTHER

_____   _____

_____   _____

_____   _____

Consider these questions as you look over your activities:

- How could you use your regular activities to engage the people in your Spheres of Influence? Look for things you can do with an unbeliever instead of doing them by yourself.

- Do you need to remove any activities that keep you from engaging the people in your Spheres of Influence?

- Do you need to add any activities that would give you more opportunities to engage the people in your Spheres of Influence?

Get Ready for Group

Write your memorized Scripture.

_____

_____

_____

_____

_____

What observations and interpretations of Scripture were most meaningful to you?

_____

_____

_____

_____

_____

Summarize your key takeaway(s) for this week.

_____

_____

_____

_____

_____

What will you tell the group about the results of your exercise this week?

_____

_____

_____

_____

_____

How has this week helped you better understand and apply the Spiritual Growth Grid?

_____

_____

_____

_____

_____

	REPENT & BELIEVE		
WHO GOD IS	WHAT GOD DID	WHO WE ARE	WHAT WE DO
KING	CALLED	CITIZENS	LISTEN & OBEY
FATHER	ADOPTED	FAMILY	LOVE & SERVE
SAVIOR	SENT	MISSIONARIES	GO & MULTIPLY

05

MISSIONAL PRESENCE

SCRIPTURE MEMORY

For God so loved the world, that he
gave his only Son, that whoever believes in him should not perish but
have eternal life.

—*John 3:16*

LISTEN

Scripture Study

LUKE 15:1-2

Now the tax collectors and sinners were all drawing near to hear him. ²And the Pharisees and the scribes grumbled, saying, "This man receives sinners and eats with them."

Observing the Text

Who are the people drawing near to Jesus?

_____

_____

_____

What is the charge the religious group have against Jesus?

_____

_____

_____

Interpreting the Text

Why would the Pharisees and scribes be upset with Jesus being around "sinners"?

_____

_____

_____

What are the implications attached to "eating" with someone during that day?

_____

_____

_____

How does Jesus "receive sinners" throughout his ministry?

_____

_____

_____

Teaching

This week continues our study through the acrostic BLESS. The first letter, B, reminded us to begin with missional prayer. The next three lessons will focus on missional presence. Our missional presence will grow as we develop deeper friendships with the lost in our Spheres of Influence through three activities:

- Listen and be aware of the needs of those within your Spheres of Influence.
- Eat with those within your Spheres of Influence.
- Serve by looking for ways to engage those in your spheres with good

deeds that might open a door for the good news.

Today, let's focus on LISTEN. Listening to those within our Spheres of Influence not only will help us grow our friendships but also allow us to see where we can move those conversations toward gospel ends.

Listening well demands we become adept at asking questions. Asking questions communicates that you actually care about the person rather than seeing them as a project. It shows you value their views and really want to get to know them. You actually want to be real friends, not just acquaintances.

Asking questions can help us discover our friends' values, worldviews, fears, struggles, dreams, and spiritual perspectives. This is invaluable for sharing the good word of the gospel. With each answer you hear, you are not only getting to better know (and hopefully love) those you speak with, but also finding prospective entry points for gospel conversations in the future.

Ask open-ended questions. *What do you do for fun? What do you like about being a parent? What was your favorite childhood activity? What's the most challenging aspect of your job? What would you say is the most meaningful experience you've ever had?* Questions like these serve us well by allowing us to peer into the hearts of those we're seeking to reach.

At some point in the relationship, turn the questions to more spiritual matters. There is nothing wrong with light-hearted conversation, but many of us stay in the safety zone for too long. If missionaries are going to meaningfully converse with someone about the gospel, they need to grow more comfortable talking about the deeper things of life. The right question can make all the difference. Ask a question that intentionally causes them to think about and articulate what they really believe about life, God, people, hope, fear, and death. The goal in asking these kind of questions is to move the conversation toward what the person really believes about life's important matters. And after you ask, listen, listen, listen!

But, be careful. The temptation to immediately correct our friends concerning issues of theology and faith may arise in your heart. Fight the need to immediately become the "Answer Person" and just listen. Your role as a missionary is to take time to know those in your Spheres of Influence. Instantly correcting or countering someone's views may put unnecessary roadblocks in the relationships. They may feel you only want to preach at them instead of really getting to know them. Master the art of listening. It is the first step of having a missional presence in the lives of those we want to see embrace Christ. It's what missionaries do.

Questions for Reflection

Which aspect of this activity is most challenging for you: starting the conversation/asking questions, turning the conversation to spiritual topics, or listening without correcting or arguing? How can your group help you to grow in this area?

_____

_____

_____

When have you seen this approach make a difference in your own experience? In what ways have you seen relationships be a part of building a bridge for the gospel?

_____

_____

_____

Who within your Sphere of Influence needs to be the focus of your listening this week? What questions do you need to ask them?

_____

_____

_____

Prayer

Pray that you would be given the grace to love others with God's love and to listen with a heart for real relationships. Ask God to guide your conversations toward his gospel.

SCRIPTURE MEMORY

For God so loved the _____, that he gave his only Son, that whoever believes in him should not perish but have _____ life."

—*John 3:16*

EAT

Scripture Study

LUKE 15:1-7

Now the tax collectors and sinners were all drawing near to hear him. ² And the Pharisees and the scribes grumbled, saying, "This man receives sinners and eats with them."

³ So he told them this parable: ⁴ "What man of you, having a hundred sheep, if he has lost one of them, does not leave the ninety-nine in the open country, and go after the one that is lost, until he finds it? ⁵ And when he has found it, he lays it on his shoulders, rejoicing. ⁶ And when he comes home, he calls together his friends and his neighbors, saying to them, 'Rejoice with me, for I have found my sheep that was lost.' ⁷ Just so, I tell you, there will be more joy in heaven over one sinner who repents than over ninety-nine righteous persons who need no repentance.

Observing the text (verses 3-7)

What is a parable?

_____

_____

_____

How do we see the compassion of the sheep owner?

_____

_____

_____

How does this story intersect with the values of the kingdom of heaven?

_____

_____

_____

Interpreting the text (verses 3-7)

Why would Jesus use a parable whose background was shepherding?

_____

_____

_____

What is Jesus trying to communicate to these religious leaders in the response of the shepherd?

_____

_____

_____

What does verse 7 mean?

_____

_____

Teaching

John 1:14 highlights Jesus' humanity, saying, "And the Word became flesh and dwelt among us." The New Testament consistently witnesses Jesus making himself available to those around him. Disciples of Jesus, in the same spirit of being sent on mission, are also intentional about posturing their lives to be available to those around them for the sake of the gospel.

Living this kind of missional life requires a reorientation of our priorities. We make choices that do not primarily have our comfort in mind. Instead, we are led by the missionary activity: *go and multiply*. That may mean instead of plopping on the sofa to watch TV as soon as you get home from work, you decide to walk across the street to have a conversation with a neighbor watering the yard. We will choose activities that may be more difficult or inconvenient at times, with the goal of deepening relationships.

As we continue to pursue growing our missional presence, we turn our attention to the E of BLESS. Similarly to L (Listen), E represents another missionary activity which allows followers of Jesus to develop deeper friendships with the lost around them. What does E represent? Eat.

One of the easiest and most effective ways to develop relationships is by sharing meals with those in our Sphere of Influence. It's a simple practice which can greatly increase our missional presence. Growing numbers of pastors and Christian thought-leaders vouch for the importance of sharing meals in today's world. Missiologist Alan Hirsch writes,

> Sharing meals together on a regular basis is one of the most sacred practices we can engage in as believers. Missional hospitality is a tremendous opportunity to extend the kingdom of God. We can literally eat our way into the kingdom of God! If every Christian household regularly invited a stranger or a poor person into their home for a meal once a week, we would literally change the world by eating![1]

1 Alan Hirsch and Lance Ford, *Right Here, Right Now: Everyday Mission for Everyday People* (Grand Rapids: Baker Books, 2011), 211.

Pastors Ben Connelly and Jeff Vanderstelt highlight the fact that eating was a tool Jesus himself used. Connelly writes,

> Especially in Luke's gospel, we see Jesus eat and drink often: with tax collectors, sinners, prostitutes; with the four thousand and the five thousand; with the religious elite and the poor; with His disciples. And let's not forget his first miracle, creating lavish libation for a wedding party. Meals, water, and wine were the subject of some parables. And much of Jesus' ministry, and many significant events in His life, occurred in the context of food and drink.[2]

Vanderstelt takes Connelly's use of Jesus and eating a step further, saying,

> The table for the Jews, as also in our day, is very symbolic AND communicative – who we eat with demonstrates who we love. This is why Jesus was called a friend of sinners – he ate with people who were dirty, unreligious, and visibly or sociably unacceptable. The table is one of the most powerful displays of God's love and acceptance of sinners.[3]

Generally speaking, we eat twenty-one meals each week. That means we have more than eighty opportunities each month to fellowship with those within our Sphere of Influence over a meal. What a wonderful way to redeem our days for the mission of God!

Invite your unbelieving friends for a meal at your house, grab a bite for lunch with your co-workers at a nearby restaurant, or have a cookout for the neighborhood. Missionaries leverage their meals for the kingdom

2 Ben Connelly and Bob Roberts Jr., *A Field Guide for Everyday Mission: 30 Days and 101 Ways to Demonstrate the Gospel* (Chicago: Moody Publishers, 2014), 124.
3 Jeff Vanderstelt, *Soma School Notes*, 16.

of God. Eating—it's one way we can both deepen our relationships and BLESS those in our Spheres of Influence.

Questions for Reflection

In what ways do you need to reorient your life to reflect missional priorities—choosing interaction and support over comfort or convenience?

_____

_____

_____

How have you seen relationships grow and develop around a table?

_____

_____

_____

Who can you eat with this week to leverage your meals for the kingdom of God?

_____

_____

_____

Prayer

Thank Jesus for coming to earth as a human and embracing those who were far from him, including you. Ask him to help you to pursue intimate involvement in the lives of the lost, even when it is inconvenient or uncomfortable for you.

SCRIPTURE MEMORY

For _____ so loved the world, that he _____ his only Son, that _____ believes in him should not perish but have eternal life.

—John 3:16

SERVE

Scripture Study

LUKE 15:1-10

Now the tax collectors and sinners were all drawing near to hear him. [2] And the Pharisees and the scribes grumbled, saying, "This man receives sinners and eats with them."

[3] So he told them this parable: [4] "What man of you, having a hundred sheep, if he has lost one of them, does not leave the ninety-nine in the open country, and go after the one that is lost, until he finds it? [5] And when he has found it, he lays it on his shoulders, rejoicing. [6] And when he comes home, he calls together his friends and his neighbors, saying to them, 'Rejoice with me, for I have found my sheep that was lost.' [7] Just so, I tell you, there will be more joy in heaven over one sinner who repents than over ninety-nine righteous persons who need no repentance.

[8] "Or what woman, having ten silver coins, if she loses one coin, does not light a lamp and sweep the house and seek diligently until she finds it? [9] And when she has found it, she calls together her friends and neighbors, saying, 'Rejoice with me, for I have found the coin that I had lost.' [10] Just so, I tell you, there is joy before the angels of God over one sinner who repents."

Observing the Text (verses 8-10)

What is the object of value in this second parable and how is it sought?

_____

_____

_____

How is the response of the woman in this parable like the response of the shepherd in the previous parable?

_____

_____

_____

According to Jesus, what is the point of the parable?

_____

_____

_____

Interpreting the Text

Why does Jesus stress that the woman will "light a lamp and sweep the house and seek diligently until she finds" the lost coin?

_____

_____

_____

What is the meaning behind the same responses for both woman and shepherd upon finding what they seek?

_____

_____

_____

What does it mean to be "one who repents"?

_____

_____

_____

Teaching

When the mother of two disciples asked Jesus if he would grant her sons places of power and prestige in his kingdom, Christ responded by explaining what his kingdom truly values:

> You know that the rulers of the Gentiles lord it over them, and their great ones exercise authority over them. It shall not be so among you. But whoever would be great among you must be your servant, and whoever would be first among you must be your slave, even as the Son of Man came not to be served but to serve, and to give his life as a ransom for many.
>
> Matthew 20:25-28

Servanthood is the great value in God's economy. Jesus defined his own ministry as one where he came "not to be served but to serve." Indeed, he demonstrated the ultimate service of others by giving "his life as a ransom" for sinners at the Cross. Christ led by serving.

So far this week we've looked at the L and E of BLESS. Today, we examine the last activity of missional presence that seeks to develop deeper, meaningful friendships within our Spheres of Influence. It is represented by the first S, which stands for Serve. Missionaries, armed with a new purpose to go and multiply, seek opportunities to serve those within their Spheres of Influence.

This spirit of servanthood isn't just a hallmark of how the church treats itself (see 1 Corinthians 12) but how it should engage the world. Jesus teaches in Matthew 5:

> You are the salt of the earth, but if salt has lost its taste, how shall its saltiness be restored? It is no longer good for anything except to be thrown out and trampled under people's feet. You are the light of the world. A city set on a hill cannot be hidden. Nor do people light a lamp and put it under a basket, but on a stand, and it gives light to all in the house. In the same way, let your light shine before others, so that they may see your good works and give glory to your Father who is in heaven.
>
> Matthew 5:13-16

Christ expects the church to shine for God and his kingdom in the dark world around us. It does that by, not only sharing the word of the gospel, but also showing the world how the gospel changes our hearts to love others. Jesus demonstrated that we love others well by serving them. In doing so, our "good works" have the potential to open doors for the good news!

Missionaries know living intentionally before a watching world means serving that world in a way that demonstrates to all that Christians are a part of a different kingdom – God's kingdom. This is the power of serving those in your Spheres of Influence: we can increase our gospel influence amongst our neighbors, friends, and others who need the gift of Jesus. The Reformer Martin Luther said, "It is the duty of every Christian to be Christ to his neighbor."[1] The question then is clear: how can followers of Jesus serve their neighbors well?

---

1 Martin Luther, *Concerning Christian Liberty*.

The possibilities are endless. Look for the needs of those around you and see how you can practically and lovingly meet those needs. Here are some ideas:

- Mentor at-risk youth for one hour each week.
- Mow the yard of your elderly neighbors.
- Be a listening ear to co-workers who are feeling the pressure of their work.
- Support a foster family by becoming certified to provide respite child care.
- Deliver a meal to a busy neighbor or a family battling a serious illness.
- Join with a local mission partner that seeks the welfare of the city (e.g., a pregnancy center, anti-human trafficking groups, homeless ministries).

Missionaries understand the impact behind the "good deeds" of service for the gospel's sake. They know serving others strengthens the relationships within our Spheres of Influence. They also realize that, combined with listening and eating, a missionary who serves can effectively increase his or her missional presence to go and multiply.

Questions for Reflection
Do you believe that servanthood holds the greatest value in God's economy? How do you see this reflected in the church today? In your own attitude?

_____

_____

_____

How have you seen believers serving in a way that gives a light for the gospel to the world around them?

_____

_____

In what ways can you serve those within your Sphere of Influence in order to meet their needs and increase your gospel influence?

_____

_____

_____

Prayer

Pray that your group and our church would serve others in a way that would attract others to Jesus and his gospel. Ask God to open your eyes and soften your heart to opportunities to serve those within your Sphere of Influence.

WEEKLY
EXERCISE

MISSIONAL PRESENCE

In the next seven days find a way to employ one of the three activities in order to be a better missional presence to those in your Spheres of Influence. Then write up an account of what happened. Circle one of the following:

- Listen and be aware of the needs of those within your Spheres of Influence.
- Eat with those within your Spheres of Influence.
- Serve by looking for ways to engage those in your spheres with good deeds that might open a door for the good news.

THE REPORT OF ACTIVITY:

_____

_____

_____

_____

_____

_____

_____

_____

_____

_____

_____

_____

_____

_____

_____

_____

_____

Get Ready for Group

Write your memorized Scripture.

_____

_____

_____

_____

_____

What observations and interpretations of Scripture were most meaningful to you?

_____

_____

_____

_____

_____

Summarize your key takeaway(s) for this week.

_____

_____

_____

_____

_____

What will you tell the group about the results of your exercise this week?

_____

_____

_____

_____

How has this week helped you better understand and apply the Spiritual Growth Grid?

_____

_____

_____

_____

_____

06

GOSPEL CONVERSATIONS

SCRIPTURE MEMORY

For God so loved the world, that he gave his only Son, that whoever believes in him should not perish but have eternal life.

—John 3:16

BEFORE THE CONVERSATION BEGINS

Scripture Study

LUKE 15:11-32

And he said, "There was a man who had two sons. [12] And the younger of them said to his father, 'Father, give me the share of property that is coming to me.' And he divided his property between them. [13] Not many days later, the younger son gathered all he had and took a journey into a far country, and there he squandered his property in reckless living. [14] And when he had spent everything, a severe famine arose in that country, and he began to be in need. [15] So he went and hired himself out to one of the citizens of that country, who sent him into his fields to feed pigs. [16] And he was longing to be fed with the pods that the pigs ate, and no one gave him anything.

[17] "But when he came to himself, he said, 'How many of my father's hired servants have more than enough bread, but I perish here with hunger! [18] I will arise and go to my father, and I will say to him, "Father, I have sinned against heaven and before you. [19] I am no longer worthy to be called your son. Treat me as one of your hired servants."' [20] And he arose and came to his father. But while he was still a long way off, his father saw him and

felt compassion, and ran and embraced him and kissed him. ²¹ And the son said to him, 'Father, I have sinned against heaven and before you. I am no longer worthy to be called your son.' ²² But the father said to his servants, 'Bring quickly the best robe, and put it on him, and put a ring on his hand, and shoes on his feet. ²³ And bring the fattened calf and kill it, and let us eat and celebrate. ²⁴ For this my son was dead, and is alive again; he was lost, and is found.' And they began to celebrate.

²⁵ "Now his older son was in the field, and as he came and drew near to the house, he heard music and dancing. ²⁶ And he called one of the servants and asked what these things meant. ²⁷ And he said to him, 'Your brother has come, and your father has killed the fattened calf, because he has received him back safe and sound.' ²⁸ But he was angry and refused to go in. His father came out and entreated him, ²⁹ but he answered his father, 'Look, these many years I have served you, and I never disobeyed your command, yet you never gave me a young goat, that I might celebrate with my friends. ³⁰ But when this son of yours came, who has devoured your property with prostitutes, you killed the fattened calf for him!' ³¹ And he said to him, 'Son, you are always with me, and all that is mine is yours. ³² It was fitting to celebrate and be glad, for this your brother was dead, and is alive; he was lost, and is found.'"

Observing the Text

Which of the sons demanded the inheritance, and what was the father's response?

_____

_____

_____

How would you characterize the younger son's experience after leaving home?

_____

_____

_____

How do verses 15-16 tell us how bad things got for this son?

_____

_____

_____

Interpreting the Text

What was so egregious about the younger son's actions?

_____

_____

_____

How is this contrast between before and after supposed to strike the reader?

_____

_____

_____

Teaching

Let's review. In order to BLESS others in our Spheres of Influence we:

- Begin with prayer
- Listen

- Eat
- Serve

That leaves us with the final "S" which stands for Share. Missionaries trust their new, God-given purpose in life is fulfilled by sharing the gospel with the world around them. It is important to consider four characteristics which must be present in our lives if we are going to faithfully point others to Christ. They set the tone for us before we ever say a word to another person. In moving from missional presence to a missional proclamation we should:

Pursue God daily

The great gift of the gospel is that in Christ we have been brought near to God—we have access to him (Ephesians 2:17-18; 1 Peter 3:18). And because of his undeserved favor and kindness toward us, we can't help but desire a deeper relationship with him. Psalm 84:1-2 says:

> How lovely is Your dwelling place, O Lord of hosts! My soul longs, yes, faints for the courts of the Lord; my heart and flesh sing for joy to the living God.

Remember, apart from Christ we can do nothing, but in him we will bear much fruit (John 15:1-11). Missional proclamation is meant to flow from our relationship with God. Let us not share about the God we've only heard about, but the God we know personally. Pursuing a vibrant walk with God cannot be stressed enough.

Trust the Holy Spirit

In John 16, Jesus describes the work of the Holy Spirit: convicting the world of sin, righteousness and judgment, guiding believers into the truth, and pointing people to Jesus Christ (John 16:7-15). The Spirit of God has also empowered you to be his witness to the world around you (Acts 1:8).

Jesus promised believers the power to proclaim the gospel, assuring them that their words would be "the Spirit of the Father speaking through you" (Matthew 10:19-20).

Be careful not to prejudge whether people are interested in the things of God. We have no idea what the Holy Spirit may doing in people's hearts, no matter what they display on the outside.

Be ourselves

Gospel proclamation is not meant to be done with a certain personality or style. Use your unique spiritual gifts, personality, and talents. The people in your sphere know you. As you begin to step out, have confidence in the power and leading of the Holy Spirit. He can shape you into a faithful witness.

Understand the power and the sufficiency of Scripture

In Psalm 19:7-9, David writes:

> *The law of the Lord is perfect, reviving the soul; the testimony of the Lord is sure, making wise the simple; the precepts of the Lord are right, rejoicing the heart; the commandment of the Lord is pure, enlightening the eyes; the fear of the Lord is clean, enduring forever; the rules of the Lord are true, and righteous altogether.*

These verses tell us that the word of God is perfect, sure, right, pure, true, and righteous. God uses his word to revive the soul, make us wise, bring us joy, and give light to our eyes. Isaiah also reminds us of the power of God's word:

> *For as the rain and the snow come down from heaven and do not return there but water the earth, making it bring forth and*

sprout, giving seed to the sower and bread to the eater, so shall
my word be that goes out from my mouth; it shall not return
to me empty, but it shall accomplish that which I purpose, and
shall succeed in the thing for which I sent it.

Isaiah 55:10-11

God will accomplish what he wants in the sharing of his word. Sharing the message of the gospel will be fruitful in one way or another, whether we immediately see results or not. Either way, God is in control and his word is powerful, authoritative, and sufficient to accomplish his will. If we are going to have a meaningful gospel conversation, it must be centered on the Scriptures, for they alone are God-breathed (2 Timothy 3:16).

As we share with others, remember to put God's word in the teaching position. We do not want to take an "us versus them" mentality. The message we bring is not ours but God's. We desire only that our unbelieving friends take what it says seriously and consider what their response to it might be. Missionaries know that before they ever open their mouths to share, they are first committed to maturing spiritually by pursuing God daily, trusting in the Holy Spirit, being themselves, and valuing Scripture.

Questions for Reflection

Are you pursuing God daily? Why do you think this is essential to the life of a missionary?

_____

_____

_____

When it comes to sharing the gospel, what type of personality is valued by the church? How has this mindset encouraged or discouraged you from sharing? How can you utilize your uniqueness to be a witness to those in your Sphere of Influence?

_____

_____

_____

In what ways do you struggle to believe that God's word can bring about his will?

_____

_____

_____

Prayer

Praise God for the work of his Spirit and the sufficiency of his word in accomplishing the spread of the gospel throughout the world. Thank him that he allows us to participate in this task, and ask him to daily draw you to himself and equip you to share the gospel.

SCRIPTURE MEMORY

For God so loved the world, that he gave his _____, that whoever believes in him _____ but have eternal life.

—*John 3:16*

ASKING THE RIGHT QUESTIONS

Scripture Study

LUKE 15:11-32

And he said, "There was a man who had two sons. *¹²* And the younger of them said to his father, 'Father, give me the share of property that is coming to me.' And he divided his property between them. *¹³* Not many days later, the younger son gathered all he had and took a journey into a far country, and there he squandered his property in reckless living. *¹⁴* And when he had spent everything, a severe famine arose in that country, and he began to be in need. *¹⁵* So he went and hired himself out to one of the citizens of that country, who sent him into his fields to feed pigs. *¹⁶* And he was longing to be fed with the pods that the pigs ate, and no one gave him anything.

¹⁷ "But when he came to himself, he said, 'How many of my father's hired servants have more than enough bread, but I perish here with hunger! *¹⁸* I will arise and go to my father, and I will say to him, "Father, I have sinned against heaven and before you. *¹⁹* I am no longer worthy to be called your son. Treat me as one of your hired servants."' *²⁰* And he arose and came to his father. But while he was still a long way off, his father saw him and felt compassion, and ran and embraced him and kissed him. *²¹* And the son said to him, 'Father, I have sinned against heaven and before you. I am no longer worthy to be called your son.' [22] But the father said to his servants, 'Bring quickly the best robe, and put it on him, and put a ring on his hand, and shoes on his feet. [23] And bring the fattened calf and kill it, and let us eat and celebrate. [24] For this my son was dead, and is alive again; he was lost, and is found.' And they began to celebrate.

[25] "Now his older son was in the field, and as he came and drew near to the house, he heard music and dancing. [26] And he called one of the servants and asked what these things meant. [27] And he said to him, 'Your brother has come, and your father has killed the fattened calf, because he has received him back safe and sound.' [28] But he was angry and refused to go in. His father came out and entreated him, [29] but he answered his father, 'Look, these many years I have served you, and I never disobeyed your command, yet you never gave me a young goat, that I might celebrate with my friends. [30] But when this son of yours came, who has devoured your property with prostitutes, you killed the fattened calf for him!' [31] And he said to him, 'Son, you are always with me, and all that is mine is yours. [32] It was fitting to celebrate and be glad, for this your brother was dead, and is alive; he was lost, and is found.'"

Observing the text (verses 17-24)

What phrase or phrases describes the younger son's repentance?

_____

_____

_____

Who does the son believe he has sinned against?

_____

_____

_____

What is the father's response to the younger son?

_____

_____

_____

Interpreting the text (verses 17-24)

Why would the younger son say he has sinned against the father and God (i.e., heaven)?

_____

_____

_____

What does the father's response tell us about God's heart for sinners?

_____

_____

_____

How is the celebration for the son an act of grace?

_____

_____

_____

Teaching

The previous lesson addressed what we do prior to initiating a gospel conversation with those in our Sphere of Influence. Now comes the moment when we turn the conversation toward matters of faith. When that happens it's time to employ the last letter of BLESS—we Share. How do we go from showing love and grace (by serving) to proclaiming love and grace (by sharing)? We begin by asking the right questions and listening to their answers. While we talked about the importance of good questions earlier in this study, the questions at this point in the conversation are doorways to spiritual conversations.

The right kind of question can make all the difference. Will you ask a question that intentionally causes those in your Sphere of Influence to articulate what they believe about deeper things—God, people, hope, fear, death, and eternity? There is nothing wrong with light-hearted conversation, but many of us remain there far too long. If we are going to meaningfully converse with someone about the gospel, we need to grow more comfortable talking about the serious matters of life and living.

Here are some good potential questions:
- What is your spiritual background?
- How do you find comfort in difficult times?
- What will it take for you to be at rest from your anxiety?
- With all of this brokenness around us, do you think there is any hope of things getting better?
- Where do you think we come from? Why do we exist?
- Do you think we are all inherently good? Why or why not?
- What is your understanding of the gospel message?
- Who do you think Jesus is?
- Where do you find your ultimate hope?
- Has there been a time in your life where it seemed as if God was not there for you when you really needed Him to be? (This is a great question to ask of someone who seems angry toward God, church, or spiritual things.)

The goal is asking questions which move the conversation toward what the person really believes about God. Don't be too discouraged if you find someone who isn't interested in talking about spiritual things. Pray for them, asking God to send his Spirit to open their heart and mind to spiritual conversations and the gospel itself. Don't stop asking the right questions. Missionaries keep asking for as long as it takes!

Questions for Reflection

When have you struggled to start a gospel conversation with someone in your Sphere of Influence? What fears or concerns tend to hold you back?

_____

_____

_____

What questions have you utilized to bring a conversation to a deeper level? How have those experiences gone for you?

_____

_____

_____

What relationship in your life needs to make the turn from surface conversation to a gospel opportunity? What do you need to do to make that intentional shift? How can your group help?

_____

_____

_____

Prayer

Pray that God would give you wisdom to shift your conversations with the right spiritual questions. Ask him to prepare the hearts of those in your Sphere of Influence with a curiosity about the gospel and a desire for deeper truths.

SCRIPTURE MEMORY

For God _____, that he gave his only Son, that whoever believes in him should not perish ___ _____.

—*John 3:16*

SHARING YOUR STORY

Scripture Study

LUKE 15:11-32

And he said, "There was a man who had two sons. ¹² And the younger of them said to his father, 'Father, give me the share of property that is coming to me.' And he divided his property between them. ¹³ Not many days later, the younger son gathered all he had and took a journey into a far country, and there he squandered his property in reckless living. ¹⁴ And when he had spent everything, a severe famine arose in that country, and he began to be in need. ¹⁵ So he went and hired himself out to one of the citizens of that country, who sent him into his fields to feed pigs. ¹⁶ And he was longing to be fed with the pods that the pigs ate, and no one gave him anything.

¹⁷ "But when he came to himself, he said, 'How many of my father's hired servants have more than enough bread, but I perish here with hunger! ¹⁸ I will arise and go to my father, and I will say to him, "Father, I have sinned against heaven and before you. ¹⁹ I am no longer worthy to be called your son. Treat me as one of your hired servants."' ²⁰ And he arose and came to his father. But while he was still a long way off, his father saw him and felt compassion, and ran and embraced him and kissed him. *21 And the son said to him, 'Father, I have sinned against heaven and before you. I am no longer worthy to be called your son.' 22 But the father said to his servants, 'Bring quickly the best robe, and put it on him, and put a ring on his hand, and shoes on his feet. 23 And bring the fattened calf and kill it, and let us eat and celebrate. 24 For this my son was dead, and is alive again; he was lost, and is found.' And they began to celebrate.*

25 "Now his older son was in the field, and as he came and drew near to the house, he heard music and dancing. 26 And he called one of the servants and asked what these things meant. 27 And he said to him, 'Your brother has come, and your father has killed the fattened calf, because he has received him back safe and sound.' 28 But he was angry and refused to go in. His father came out and entreated him, 29 but he answered his father, 'Look, these many years I have served you, and I never disobeyed your command, yet you never gave me a young goat, that I might celebrate with my friends. 30 But when this son of yours came, who has devoured your property with prostitutes, you killed the fattened calf for him!' 31 And he said to him, 'Son, you are always with me, and all that is mine is yours. 32 It was fitting to celebrate and be glad, for this your brother was dead, and is alive; he was lost, and is found.'"

Observing the Text (verses 25-32)

What is the response of the older son?

_____

_____

_____

How does the older son explain his anger to his father?

_____

_____

_____

What is the father's rationale for the festivities?

_____

_____

_____

Interpreting the Text (verses 25-32)

Why does Jesus introduce the older son in the parable? Who does he represent of the listeners in Luke 15?

_____

_____

_____

Why does the father believe his celebration is worth it and that the older son should join in?

_____

_____

_____

Why would Jesus conclude this section on 'Lost Things' in light of the accusation of Luke 15:2, "And the Pharisees and the scribes grumbled, saying, 'This man receives sinners and eats with them.'"?

_____

_____

_____

Teaching

Today concludes our discussion of how we can BLESS those in our Spheres of Influence when we Share the gospel. This week we have spoken about personal preparation for sharing the gospel and how we should genuinely learn about those in our Sphere by initiating conversations, asking questions, and listening for windows of opportunity to enter gospel waters. One way that can happen is by sharing our own journey—how the gospel has impacted our lives.

Missionaries should be prepared to share their own stories of God's work in response to questions those in their Spheres of Influence may ask. How has God's word given you comfort, direction, and given you hope? How did God draw you to Himself?

We might turn a conversation this way:

This was my life before Christ: _____.

This is my life now: _____.

Here's how Jesus made the difference: _____.

Here are some questions about your past to help you think through sharing your faith story:
- Who were you before you met Christ?
- How did you become convicted of your sin?
- When did you embrace the work of Christ on the cross?
- How has embracing Christ changed your life?
- What caused you to seek after Christ?

Now, think through these questions about your current walk with Jesus:
- How has God demonstrated his faithfulness to you?
- How has God's Word shown itself to be true?
- How has the gospel affected your view on life in the midst of difficult circumstances?
- Why do you and/or your family do the things you do and make the

decisions you make?

- How has God used his people to bless you?

If the person you are engaging begins to ask questions and shows genuine interest in spiritual things, keep the conversation going! Make sure your questions and story keep pointing toward Christ. In the same way, make sure your answers rest on Scripture, because they ultimately point to Christ as well.

Depending on how your conversations go, you might consider pointing them to a resource. This provides a great way for those in your Spheres of Influence to process the claims of the gospel on their own. It is also a great way to continue the conversation. You can set up a time to review what they read and their thoughts about it. Here are some suggested resources:

- The Gospel of John
- *The Reason For God* or *Making Sense of God* by Tim Keller
- *What Is The Gospel?* by Greg Gilbert
- *Mere Christianity* by C.S. Lewis

These resources and the conversations we have around them are ultimately meant to help lead those in our spheres into a relationship with God. Remember, Jesus began his conversation with the woman at the well with the end in mind being himself. His goal was to draw that lady to himself and the truth of who he was. This needs to be our purpose as well. Missionaries ultimately seek to lead others in their spheres to the person and work of Jesus Christ. The goal of missional proclamation is Jesus and the good news of the gospel.

It is possible that even if this makes sense to you, you still find yourself with a lot of reasons why you cannot do it. There is a good chance the main thing holding you back is fear. We can seek to overcome this with three reminders:

1. *Relax:* It is not up to you save those in your Spheres of Influence. Salvation is solely God's job. (2 Corinthians 4:1-6, John 4:41-44)
2. *Invest:* Our investment is in the relationship, not an outcome.
3. *Remember:* If they reject the gospel, they are not rejecting you but Jesus. (John 15:18-16:4)

People are more interested in spiritual things than we often give them credit. But, it is important to remember we cannot be in a hurry with these things. We need to let the conversation develop; bad things can happen when we are in too much of a hurry. It takes time to build the relationship. Nevertheless, may we live with a sense of urgency that fosters an intentionality to share with others but still leaves room for patience.

Missionaries BLESS others! It's the way we can live out our new gospel mission of going and multiplying.

Questions for Reflection

When have you shared your story with someone else? Why was this difficult (or not) for you?

_____

_____

_____

What specific resources could you use to share with those within your Sphere of Influence? Who might be open to studying something like this with you?

_____

_____

_____

Which component of BLESS is most challenging for you? How can your group support your commitment to grow in that area?

_____

_____

_____

Prayer

Ask God to open your eyes to opportunities for sharing your story with those in your Sphere of Influence. Pray that he would take away your fear and give you a sense of urgency.

WEEKLY EXERCISE

BUILDING A BRIDGE

Write five questions that would be good bridges to a spiritual conversation with someone in your Spheres of Influence.

1. _____
   _____
   _____
   _____

2. _____
   _____
   _____
   _____

3. _____
   _____
   _____
   _____

4. _____
   _____
   _____
   _____

5. _____
   _____
   _____
   _____

Get Ready for Group

Write your memorized Scripture.

_____

_____

_____

_____

_____

What observations and interpretations of Scripture were most meaningful to you?

_____

_____

_____

_____

_____

Summarize your key takeaway(s) for this week.

_____

_____

_____

_____

_____

What will you tell the group about the results of your exercise this week?

_____

_____

_____

_____

_____

How has this week helped you better understand and apply the Spiritual Growth Grid?

_____

_____

_____

_____

_____

REPENT & BELIEVE			
WHO GOD IS	WHAT GOD DID	WHO WE ARE	WHAT WE DO
KING	CALLED	CITIZENS	LISTEN & OBEY
FATHER	ADOPTED	FAMILY	LOVE & SERVE
SAVIOR	SENT	MISSIONARIES	GO & MULTIPLY

07

THE PURPOSE OF OUR GRACE STORY

SCRIPTURE MEMORY

For the wages of sin is death, but the free gift of God is eternal life in Christ Jesus our Lord.

—*Romans 6:23*

THE IMPORTANCE OF OUR GRACE STORY

Scripture Study

JOHN 9:1-7

As he passed by, he saw a man blind from birth. ² And his disciples asked him, "Rabbi, who sinned, this man or his parents, that he was born blind?" ³ Jesus answered, "It was not that this man sinned, or his parents, but that the works of God might be displayed in him. ⁴ We must work the works of him who sent me while it is day; night is coming, when no one can work. ⁵ As long as I am in the world, I am the light of the world." ⁶ Having said these things, he spit on the ground and made mud with the saliva. Then he anointed the man's eyes with the mud ⁷ and said to him, "Go, wash in the pool of Siloam" (which means Sent). So he went and washed and came back seeing.

Observing the Text

Who are the main characters in this passage?

_____

_____

_____

What is the question asked when faced with someone's disability?

_____

_____

_____

What was Jesus response?

_____

_____

_____

Interpreting the Text

What does this say about how people viewed physical ailments or disabilities from a theological perspective?

_____

_____

Why would Jesus refer to himself as the Light of the World based on the context?

_____

_____

_____

What do you make of Jesus' way to heal the man's eyes?

_____

_____

_____

Teaching

Our stories are very important. As God writes his grace into each of our lives, he does so in the midst of a lost world in need of redemption. Every follower of Jesus Christ has been covered by God's grace, brought from death to life, and now lives with an eternal hope in a reconciled relationship with the Almighty God. But, as we live this life, we are surrounded by people who do not have this kind of existence in Christ. In Ephesians 2:12, Paul describes who we once were, admonishing believers to "remember that you were at that time separated from Christ... having no hope and without God in the world," providing a clear contrast with what we have been graciously given in Jesus.

We cannot separate our new lives in Christ (our gospel identity) from God's mission (our gospel activity). We are his ambassadors who have been entrusted with the message of reconciliation (2 Corinthians 5:17-21). God wants to use us, as missionaries, to declare his salvation to those in our Spheres of Influence. Our stories—the narratives of how our lives have been intersected by the gospel of Jesus—play a major role in this proclamation. As those who have been reconciled, it is essential for us to understand the importance of our own journey.

Sadly, many Christians downplay their stories, feeling they don't measure up or may even bore people. In reality, everyone's story of salvation is significant. Your story, personally, and our story, corporately, come together to play an important role in declaring the gospel to the world around us. This is a powerful thing because it shows how God saved us, made us alive, and continues to walk with us in this life. What could possibly be unimportant, boring, or insignificant about any of that?

The remaining weeks will continue to train you as a missionary by focusing on missional proclamation: the purpose of your story, building your story, and sharing your story. Our hope is that you'll be better prepared as a missionary, ready to share the gospel in word and deed with those in your Spheres of Influence using the story God has given to you.

Questions for Reflection

Do you have a sense that your story is worth telling? Why or why not?

_____

_____

_____

Like the woman at the well in John 4, do you feel a sense of excitement to tell your story to those around you? Why or why not?

_____

_____

_____

What hinders you from actively looking to share your story as often as you can? What does your fear reveal about your beliefs about God's character and your faith in his promises?

_____

_____

_____

Prayer

Thank God that he has changed you from the inside-out and given you a Grace Story to tell. Pray that he would give you the boldness to share that story within your Spheres of Influence.

SCRIPTURE MEMORY

For the wages of ___ is death, but the ___ gift of God is eternal life in Christ Jesus our Lord.

—Romans 6:23

BEGINNING WITH THE END IN MIND

Scripture Study

JOHN 9:1-12

As he passed by, he saw a man blind from birth. ² And his disciples asked him, "Rabbi, who sinned, this man or his parents, that he was born blind?" ³ Jesus answered, "It was not that this man sinned, or his parents, but that the works of God might be displayed in him. ⁴ We must work the works of him who sent me while it is day; night is coming, when no one can work. ⁵ As long as I am in the world, I am the light of the world." ⁶ Having said these things, he spit on the ground and made mud with the saliva. Then he anointed the man's eyes with the mud ⁷ and said to him, "Go, wash in the pool of Siloam" (which means Sent). So he went and washed and came back seeing.

⁸ The neighbors and those who had seen him before as a beggar were saying, "Is this not the man who used to sit and beg?" ⁹ Some said, "It is he." Others said, "No, but he is like him." He kept saying, "I am the man." ¹⁰So they said to him, "Then how were your eyes opened?" ¹¹ He answered, "The man called Jesus made mud and anointed my eyes and said to me, 'Go to Siloam and wash.' So I went and washed and received my sight."

[12]They said to him, "Where is he?" He said, "I do not know."

Observing the text (verses 8-12)

Who is impacted immediately by this miracle?

_____

_____

_____

What is the question they put to the healed man?

_____

_____

_____

What is the man's response?

_____

_____

_____

Interpreting the text (verses 8-12)

Why would the people naturally respond the way they do at the beginning?

_____

_____

_____

How would you describe the man's response to the questions of his neighbors?

_____

_____

_____

Teaching

For what we proclaim is not ourselves, but Jesus Christ as Lord,
with ourselves as your servants for Jesus' sake.

2 Corinthians 4:5

What is the reason for sharing our Grace Story? If we are not careful, people can easily walk away after hearing our testimony with something other than what God intended. At times our stories can sound like we have bought into a self-improvement plan. We say things like:

- "I was this way, and now I am this way..."
- "I used to do this, but now I don't..."
- "I used to feel this way, and now I feel this way..."
- "I thought this way about myself, but now I see things differently..."
- "I was going through a really difficult time, and here's how Jesus got me out of it..."

While these examples do play an important part in our stories, they cannot be left in isolation, inaccurately framing the gospel and Jesus himself as a mere tool you found to benefit your life. This "fixed me" type of presentation can open the door for responses like: "I am very happy that has worked for you; here is what I have found", "Here's what I do to get that same outcome (with even better results than you)", or "I'm happy with my own way; it works for me." When our stories present Jesus as a great life-manager, personal happiness genie, or Mr. Fix-It, instead of the one true Lord and Savior, we create unnecessary barriers to the real gospel in the hearts and minds of listeners.

At the end of John's gospel, he reminds his reader that it was written with a purpose: "so that you may believe that Jesus is the Christ, the Son of

God, and that by believing you may have life in his name" (John 20:31). The endgame of our story should mirror this objective, governing what we say and how we say it. Ideally, listeners should leave thinking that what they've heard has implications for them. Our Grace Stories can be brilliant declarations of Chris—what he has done, is doing, and continues to do in our lives. They can also be catalysts for deeper conversations about the gospel message. As we build and proclaim our testimonies, we must keep the end goal in mind to most effectively present Jesus to those in our Spheres of Influence.

Questions for Reflection

What important truths should be present in your Grace Story that would help point people to who Jesus is and the gospel message?

_____

_____

_____

Our culture is always looking for things that will make us happy, fix us, or help us. How does telling our Grace Stories solely from that perspective lead people into an incomplete and unhelpful view of Christ and the message of the gospel?

_____

_____

_____

Embracing Jesus does change our lives, giving us hope and abundant blessing in all circumstances. How can we declare these benefits in such a way that help point people to Christ as Lord and Savior instead of making Jesus something less than he really is?

_____

_____

_____

Prayer

Praise God that he is so much more than a tool for our happiness, but a loving Father who sent his Son to accomplish our salvation. Ask him to be evident in your words and deeds in a way that leads others to faith in him.

SCRIPTURE MEMORY

For the wages of sin is _____, but the free gift of God is _____ in Christ Jesus our Lord.

—*Romans 6:23*

EVERYONE, INCLUDING YOU

Scripture Study

JOHN 9:1-17

As he passed by, he saw a man blind from birth. ² And his disciples asked him, "Rabbi, who sinned, this man or his parents, that he was born blind?" ³ Jesus answered, "It was not that this man sinned, or his parents, but that the works of God might be displayed in him. ⁴ We must work the works of him who sent me while it is day; night is coming, when no one can work. ⁵ As long as I am in the world, I am the light of the world." ⁶ Having said these things, he spit on the ground and made mud with the saliva. Then he anointed the man's eyes with the mud ⁷ and said to him, "Go, wash in the pool of Siloam" (which means Sent). So he went and washed and came back seeing.

⁸ The neighbors and those who had seen him before as a beggar were saying, "Is this not the man who used to sit and beg?" ⁹ Some said, "It is he." Others said, "No, but he is like him." He kept saying, "I am the man." ¹⁰So they said to him, "Then how were your eyes opened?" ¹¹ He answered, "The man called Jesus made mud and anointed my eyes and said to me,

'Go to Siloam and wash.' So I went and washed and received my sight." [12] They said to him, "Where is he?" He said, "I do not know."

[13] They brought to the Pharisees the man who had formerly been blind. [14]Now it was a Sabbath day when Jesus made the mud and opened his eyes. [15] So the Pharisees again asked him how he had received his sight. And he said to them, "He put mud on my eyes, and I washed, and I see." [16] Some of the Pharisees said, "This man is not from God, for he does not keep the Sabbath." But others said, "How can a man who is a sinner do such signs?" And there was a division among them. [17] So they said again to the blind man, "What do you say about him, since he has opened your eyes?" He said, "He is a prophet."

Observing the Text (verses 12-17)

To whom is the healed man taken and what is the reason?

_____

_____

_____

How does the man's response to the Pharisees compare with the one to his neighbors?

_____

_____

_____

What puzzles the religious leaders about what has happened?

_____

_____

_____

Interpreting the Text (verses 12-17)

What bothers the Pharisees so much about this healing?

_____

_____

_____

What does this tell us about their beliefs concerning God, sickness, and sin?

_____

_____

_____

Teaching

In Mark 2, a paralyzed man is lowered him through a roof by some friends to Jesus so that he might be healed. Verse 5 says: _"And when Jesus saw their faith, he said to the paralytic, 'Son, your sins are forgiven.'"_ Then to show the crowd he had the power to forgive sins, Jesus healed the man (verses 10-12). However, the greatest gift given that day was not physical healing but spiritual healing. It was the man's sins being forgiven.

The core of our Grace Story is the same. While each of our stories may contain unique details where the Lord has transformed us in different ways, they all share the fact that we are a redeemed people. Like the paralyzed man, our sins have been forgiven in Christ! No matter what other wonderful elements may be in our stories, they all pale in comparison to this glorious truth: Jesus paid for our sin at Calvary. In that atoning work, God has forgiven us, given us the righteousness of his son, and restored us back into relationship with himself. The Bible is one big story where Jesus gets all the glory, and this should be true of your Grace Story as well. Our stories should have, at their heart, the meaning and message of Jesus' amazing work.

In fact, we should see all the other blessings we've received since coming to Christ as ultimately a result of the greatest blessing: forgiveness and restoration. The paralytic's physical blessing of being healed pointed to Christ's power to forgive him. Similarly, the blessings we receive from God point to his care for us ultimately shown in the gospel message. All of these demonstrate the goodness of God to us in Christ and are great things to share with those in our Spheres of Influence. Within each of our Grace Stories, we can share how the gospel has personally intersected our life in three parts:

- How Jesus saved us. (Past Grace Story)
- How this gift impacts us every day. (Present Grace Story)
- How this grace enables us to live with hope. (Future Grace Story)

We are going to spend the remaining weeks looking at a series of thoughts and questions that center around how the gospel has been woven into our lives in the past, present, and future. The foundation of all this is the gospel truth that our sin has been forgiven and we now have a reconciled relationship with God. May this gospel be imprinted on our hearts, deepening and strengthening our missional proclamation to those within our Spheres of Influence.

Questions for Reflection

How can forgiveness influence the life and relationships of both the one who sinned and one who was sinned against?

_____

_____

_____

What do you think it looks like to live every day in light of God's forgiveness? Why is this important for us to understand, especially when it comes to our Grace Story?

_____

_____

_____

How can we actively seek to keep God's forgiveness always in front of us?

_____

_____

Prayer

Thank Jesus for his willing death on the cross for our salvation. Pray that God would remind you continually of the goodness of his forgiveness and help you to proclaim it to others.

WEEKLY EXERCISE

BUILDING YOUR PERSONAL
SALVATION STORY

Answer these questions to help build a foundation for writing your Grace Story next week.

Who were you before God saved you?

_____

_____

_____

_____

_____

What is your spiritual background? What were your beliefs about 1) God, 2) yourself (people in general), and 3) salvation?

_____

_____

_____

_____

_____

What circumstances did God step into to save you? How did he convict you of sin, convince you of his love, and point you to salvation in Christ?

_____

_____

_____

_____

What passages of Scripture did God use to show you the truth about himself, yourself (people in general), and/or salvation?

_____

_____

_____

_____

Who helped point you to Jesus? How were they influential?

_____

_____

_____

_____

_____

When and why did you embrace the work of Christ?

_____

_____

_____

_____

_____

Are there any other important details that come to mind about your salvation?

_____

_____

_____

_____

_____

Get Ready for Group

Write your memorized Scripture.

_____

_____

_____

_____

_____

What observations and interpretations of Scripture were most meaningful to you?

_____

_____

_____

_____

_____

Summarize your key takeaway(s) for this week.

_____

_____

_____

_____

_____

What will you tell the group about the results of your exercise this week?

_____

_____

_____

_____

_____

How has this week helped you better understand and apply the Spiritual Growth Grid?

_____

_____

_____

_____

_____

		REPENT & BELIEVE		
WHO GOD IS	WHAT GOD DID	WHO WE ARE	WHAT WE DO
KING	CALLED	CITIZENS	LISTEN & OBEY
FATHER	ADOPTED	FAMILY	LOVE & SERVE
SAVIOR	SENT	MISSIONARIES	GO & MULTIPLY

08

BUILDING OUR GRACE STORY

SCRIPTURE MEMORY

For the wages of sin is death, but
the free gift of God is eternal life in
Christ Jesus our Lord.

—*Romans 6:23*

OUR PAST GRACE STORY

Scripture Study

JOHN 9:1-23

As he passed by, he saw a man blind from birth. ² *And his disciples asked him, "Rabbi, who sinned, this man or his parents, that he was born blind?"* ³ *Jesus answered, "It was not that this man sinned, or his parents, but that the works of God might be displayed in him.* ⁴ *We must work the works of him who sent me while it is day; night is coming, when no one can work.* ⁵ *As long as I am in the world, I am the light of the world."* ⁶ *Having said these things, he spit on the ground and made mud with the saliva. Then he anointed the man's eyes with the mud* ⁷ *and said to him, "Go, wash in the pool of Siloam" (which means Sent). So he went and washed and came back seeing.*

⁸ *The neighbors and those who had seen him before as a beggar were saying, "Is this not the man who used to sit and beg?"* ⁹ *Some said, "It is he." Others said, "No, but he is like him." He kept saying, "I am the man."* ¹⁰*So they said to him, "Then how were your eyes opened?"* ¹¹ *He answered, "The man called Jesus made mud and anointed my eyes and said to me,*

'Go to Siloam and wash.' So I went and washed and received my sight." [12]
They said to him, "Where is he?" He said, "I do not know."

[13] *They brought to the Pharisees the man who had formerly been blind.*
[14]*Now it was a Sabbath day when Jesus made the mud and opened his
eyes.* [15] *So the Pharisees again asked him how he had received his sight.
And he said to them, "He put mud on my eyes, and I washed, and I see."*
[16] *Some of the Pharisees said, "This man is not from God, for he does not
keep the Sabbath." But others said, "How can a man who is a sinner do
such signs?" And there was a division among them.* [17] *So they said again
to the blind man, "What do you say about him, since he has opened your
eyes?" He said, "He is a prophet."*

[18] The Jews did not believe that he had been blind and had received his
sight, until they called the parents of the man who had received his sight [19]
and asked them, "Is this your son, who you say was born blind? How then
does he now see?" [20] His parents answered, "We know that this is our son
and that he was born blind. [21] But how he now sees we do not know, nor
do we know who opened his eyes. Ask him; he is of age. He will speak for
himself." [22] (His parents said these things because they feared the Jews,
for the Jews had already agreed that if anyone should confess Jesus to be
Christ, he was to be put out of the synagogue.) [23] Therefore his parents
said, "He is of age; ask him."

Observing the Text (verses 18-23)
Who are "the Jews" based on the context of the passage?

_____

_____

_____

What is their response to this man's Grace Story?

_____

_____

_____

How do his parents answer these religious leaders?

_____

_____

_____

Interpreting the Text (verses 18-23)

Why did the religious leaders call on the man's parents?

_____

_____

_____

What do you think the parents are feeling, based on their response?

_____

_____

_____

What does this tell us about the environment's hostility to Jesus and the pressure to share one's Grace Story about Jesus?

_____

_____

_____

Teaching

As we begin to develop your grace story, let's look to the apostle Paul for an example. When he wrote to his young protégé Timothy, he shared his own story of grace:

> *I thank him who has given me strength, Christ Jesus our Lord, because he judged me faithful, appointing me to his service, though formerly I was a blasphemer, persecutor, and insolent opponent. But I received mercy because I had acted ignorantly in unbelief, and the grace of our Lord overflowed for me with the faith and love that are in Christ Jesus. The saying is trustworthy and deserving of full acceptance, that Christ Jesus came into the world to save sinners, of whom I am the foremost. But I received mercy for this reason, that in me, as the foremost, Jesus Christ might display his perfect patience as an example to those who were to believe in him for eternal life. To the King of the ages, immortal, invisible, the only God, be honor and glory forever and ever. Amen.*
>
> 1 Timothy 1:12-17

Paul tells us that he was "a blasphemer, persecutor, and insolent opponent." He acted with hostility against God in ignorance and unbelief. The apostle goes so far as to say he was the "foremost" sinner. The truth is, like Paul, all people are sinners and hostile to God. Like Paul, we are both victims and willing participants.

Looking at this example, we can begin to see ways to communicate what our lives were like before Christ's salvation changed our hearts. Here are some questions to help you frame your past:

- Who were you before God saved you?
- What were your circumstances?
- How did you demonstrate a life of ignorance and unbelief?

Notice that Paul doesn't go into great detail about his past life, but simply highlights the posture of his former self. It is important that we not dwell too much on the gritty details which might take the focus away from the goodness of God in Christ. However, people should see that we were lost like everyone else.

If you read this passage and only pay attention to the depths of Paul's sin, you've been dangerously diverted. The focus of 1 Timothy 1:12-17 is that Jesus Christ came to save sinners. Paul's life is merely an example of this glorious truth. Knowing who you were prior to your salvation is important, but more significant is the fact that you have been saved! The question we can then answer for others is, "How?"

First, our salvation was accomplished solely by Christ's death and resurrection. Paul says in 1 Corinthians 15:3-4, "For I delivered to you as of first importance what I also received: that Christ died for our sins in accordance with the Scriptures, that He was buried, that He was raised on the third day in accordance with the Scriptures." Jesus died on the cross to defeat sin and rose again in victory. When we place our trust in and follow Jesus alone as Lord and Savior, we are redeemed.

Second, God intervened in our lives with the power of the gospel. In this part, you might seek to answer these kinds of questions for your listener:

- How did God convict you of your sin, convince of you of his love, and point you to the salvation found in Jesus Christ?
- What passages of Scripture did God use?
- Who helped point you to Jesus?
- What circumstances in your life did God step into to save you?

God, in his grace, stepped into our life of sin and saved us through Jesus Christ! Our past is the story of how this happened. As important as it is to know our story, it is equally important that we are prepared to share it. Our motivation to share should ultimately be to point others to Jesus for the glory of God the Father.

Take time to think through the questions above. Write down your past grace story using these questions as your guide. Notice how clearly, fully, and concisely Paul shares his story in the 1 Timothy passage. Our personal salvation story should be able to be told in 5-7 minutes. This does not mean we will not have opportunities to share longer, but they should come as the listener asks questions. After you have written it down, look for opportunities to share it with others inside and outside the church.

Questions for Reflection

Do you feel you have a good grasp on your personal salvation story? Why or why not?

_____

_____

_____

Why should we frame our story inside the universal truth of the gospel? What does this communicate to the one who is listening?

_____

_____

_____

Why is it important not to go into too much detail about our life of sin? (This does not mean we will not have opportunities to relate to others on the deeper parts of story, but that we should be careful how we communicate our story when initially sharing.)

_____

_____

_____

Prayer

Ask God to help you to clearly see how he worked in your past to draw you to himself and to communicate this effectively as you share your grace story. Praise him for his great salvation!

SCRIPTURE MEMORY

For the _____ is death, but

the _____ is eternal life in

Christ Jesus our Lord.

—Romans 6:23

OUR PRESENT
GRACE STORY

Scripture Study

JOHN 9:1-34

As he passed by, he saw a man blind from birth. ² And his disciples asked him, "Rabbi, who sinned, this man or his parents, that he was born blind?" ³ Jesus answered, "It was not that this man sinned, or his parents, but that the works of God might be displayed in him. ⁴ We must work the works of him who sent me while it is day; night is coming, when no one can work. ⁵ As long as I am in the world, I am the light of the world." ⁶ Having said these things, he spit on the ground and made mud with the saliva. Then he anointed the man's eyes with the mud ⁷ and said to him, "Go, wash in the pool of Siloam" (which means Sent). So he went and washed and came back seeing.

⁸ The neighbors and those who had seen him before as a beggar were saying, "Is this not the man who used to sit and beg?" ⁹ Some said, "It is he." Others said, "No, but he is like him." He kept saying, "I am the man." ¹⁰So they said to him, "Then how were your eyes opened?" ¹¹ He answered, "The man called Jesus made mud and anointed my eyes and said to me,

*'Go to Siloam and wash.' So I went and washed and received my sight." *[12]
They said to him, "Where is he?" He said, "I do not know."

[13] *They brought to the Pharisees the man who had formerly been blind.*
[14] *Now it was a Sabbath day when Jesus made the mud and opened his*
eyes. [15] *So the Pharisees again asked him how he had received his sight.*
And he said to them, "He put mud on my eyes, and I washed, and I see."
[16] *Some of the Pharisees said, "This man is not from God, for he does not*
keep the Sabbath." But others said, "How can a man who is a sinner do
such signs?" And there was a division among them. [17] *So they said again*
to the blind man, "What do you say about him, since he has opened your
eyes?" He said, "He is a prophet."

[18] The Jews did not believe that he had been blind and had received his
sight, until they called the parents of the man who had received his sight
[19] and asked them, "Is this your son, who you say was born blind? How then
does he now see?" [20] His parents answered, "We know that this is our son
and that he was born blind. [21] But how he now sees we do not know, nor
do we know who opened his eyes. Ask him; he is of age. He will speak for
himself." [22] (His parents said these things because they feared the Jews,
for the Jews had already agreed that if anyone should confess Jesus to be
Christ, he was to be put out of the synagogue.) [23] Therefore his parents
said, "He is of age; ask him."

[24] *So for the second time they called the man who had been blind and*
said to him, "Give glory to God. We know that this man is a sinner." [25] *He*
answered, "Whether he is a sinner I do not know. One thing I do know,
that though I was blind, now I see." [26] *They said to him, "What did he do to*
you? How did he open your eyes?" [27] *He answered them, "I have told you*
already, and you would not listen. Why do you want to hear it again? Do
you also want to become his disciples?" [28] *And they reviled him, saying,*
"You are his disciple, but we are disciples of Moses. [29] *We know that God*

has spoken to Moses, but as for this man, we do not know where he comes from." [30] *The man answered, "Why, this is an amazing thing! You do not know where he comes from, and yet he opened my eyes.* [31] *We know that God does not listen to sinners, but if anyone is a worshiper of God and does his will, God listens to him.* [32] *Never since the world began has it been heard that anyone opened the eyes of a man born blind.* [33] *If this man were not from God, he could do nothing."* [34] *They answered him, "You were born in utter sin, and would you teach us?" And they cast him out.*

Observing the text (verses 24-34)
How do the religious leaders confront this man about Jesus a final time?

_____

_____

_____

How does the man respond, and what do the religious leaders do?

_____

_____

_____

What change do you notice in the man's last retort to these leaders?

_____

_____

_____

Interpreting the text (verses 24-34)
Why do the religious leaders think they are better because they are "disciples of Moses"?

_____

_____

_____

Why is the man's Grace Story so problematic for these leaders?

_____

_____

_____

What can we learn about their final response in verse 34 to the man's Grace Story?

_____

_____

_____

Teaching

Sharing how God saved us is one glorious aspect of our Grace Story, but the work of the gospel does not stop there. This lesson focuses on how God's grace in Christ impacts our present. We are forgiven so that we can be restored back into relationship with God. This is the ultimate good news of the gospel message. As Paul says to the Ephesians, "But now in Christ Jesus you who once were far off have been brought near by the blood of Christ" (Ephesians 2:13).

The implications of having new lives restored into relationship with the living God are many. God is faithful to his people. He continues to shape, provide for, and work through us. He lavishes grace on us and reveals himself to us. Our story is not just about a transaction of forgiveness as we go about our lives, it's about how we live for his kingdom within our restored relationship with God.

Our Grace Story illustrates not only how the gospel changed our past, but also how God's faithfulness, provision, and activity in our lives is transforming our present days. In trying to communicate your story in a clear and concise way, it may be helpful to think through the gospel storylines. God has become our heavenly father who cares for us as his children. He is our king who sovereignly leads us as his citizens through history. He is our Savior who puts our lives in a new framework of purpose and mission in life. Simply recall the goodness of the gospel to you in the here and now. For example, God is also our provider who gives us everything we need for life and godliness (2 Peter 1:3), our teacher who instructs us about righteousness, and our sanctifier who shapes us into the image of his son for his glory. And all of this doesn't even scratch the surface!

God works in wondrous ways in us, through us, for us, and around us. We must learn to recognize them. These wonderful things do not always come in huge events. They can be as simple as a family member asking for prayer who has always been hostile to the gospel. It can be learning something new about God's character as the Scriptures are read. God can demonstrate his good provision for us through another's generosity. When these blessings happen, do we recognize his care and grace? Do we take time to remember them? Do we find joy in sharing with others God's activity in our lives? These are the kind of things we can share with those in our Spheres of Influence as we get to the present section of our story. It's an important part of building your Grace Story, so spend time now thinking though and writing out how God is currently working in your life.

> *Therefore, if anyone is in Christ, he is a new creation. The old has passed away; behold, the new has come.*
>
> 2 Corinthians 5:17

Questions for Reflection

Why is it important to tether your continuing Grace Story to your restored relationship with God through Jesus Christ?

_____

_____

_____

What prevents you from taking notice of God's continuing grace in your life? What steps can you begin to take to overcome these obstacles?

_____

_____

_____

What are some practical measures you can put in place to help you remember God's faithfulness and activity?

_____

_____

_____

Prayer

Thank God for all the ways that he is actively working in you and around you every day. Pray that he would help you to recognize, remember, and tell of his goodness to those within your Spheres of Influence.

SCRIPTURE MEMORY

For the wages of sin is death, but
the free gift of God is _____

_____ our Lord.

—*Romans 6:23*

OUR FUTURE GRACE STORY

Scripture Study

JOHN 9:1-41

As he passed by, he saw a man blind from birth. ² And his disciples asked him, "Rabbi, who sinned, this man or his parents, that he was born blind?" ³ Jesus answered, "It was not that this man sinned, or his parents, but that the works of God might be displayed in him. ⁴ We must work the works of him who sent me while it is day; night is coming, when no one can work. ⁵ As long as I am in the world, I am the light of the world." ⁶ Having said these things, he spit on the ground and made mud with the saliva. Then he anointed the man's eyes with the mud ⁷ and said to him, "Go, wash in the pool of Siloam" (which means Sent). So he went and washed and came back seeing.

⁸ The neighbors and those who had seen him before as a beggar were saying, "Is this not the man who used to sit and beg?" ⁹ Some said, "It is he." Others said, "No, but he is like him." He kept saying, "I am the man." ¹⁰ o they said to him, "Then how were your eyes opened?" ¹¹ He answered, "The man called Jesus made mud and anointed my eyes and said to me,

'Go to Siloam and wash.' So I went and washed and received my sight." [12] *They said to him, "Where is he?" He said, "I do not know."*

[13] *They brought to the Pharisees the man who had formerly been blind.* [14]*Now it was a Sabbath day when Jesus made the mud and opened his eyes.* [15] *So the Pharisees again asked him how he had received his sight. And he said to them, "He put mud on my eyes, and I washed, and I see."* [16] *Some of the Pharisees said, "This man is not from God, for he does not keep the Sabbath." But others said, "How can a man who is a sinner do such signs?" And there was a division among them.* [17] *So they said again to the blind man, "What do you say about him, since he has opened your eyes?" He said, "He is a prophet."*

[18] The Jews did not believe that he had been blind and had received his sight, until they called the parents of the man who had received his sight [19]and asked them, "Is this your son, who you say was born blind? How then does he now see?" [20] His parents answered, "We know that this is our son and that he was born blind. [21] But how he now sees we do not know, nor do we know who opened his eyes. Ask him; he is of age. He will speak for himself." [22] (His parents said these things because they feared the Jews, for the Jews had already agreed that if anyone should confess Jesus to be Christ, he was to be put out of the synagogue.) [23] Therefore his parents said, "He is of age; ask him."

[24] *So for the second time they called the man who had been blind and said to him, "Give glory to God. We know that this man is a sinner."* [25] *He answered, "Whether he is a sinner I do not know. One thing I do know, that though I was blind, now I see."* [26] *They said to him, "What did he do to you? How did he open your eyes?"* [27] *He answered them, "I have told you already, and you would not listen. Why do you want to hear it again? Do you also want to become his disciples?"* [28] *And they reviled him, saying, "You are his disciple, but we are disciples of Moses.* [29] *We know that God*

has spoken to Moses, but as for this man, we do not know where he comes from." [30] The man answered, "Why, this is an amazing thing! You do not know where he comes from, and yet he opened my eyes. [31] We know that God does not listen to sinners, but if anyone is a worshiper of God and does his will, God listens to him. [32] Never since the world began has it been heard that anyone opened the eyes of a man born blind. [33] If this man were not from God, he could do nothing." [34] They answered him, "You were born in utter sin, and would you teach us?" And they cast him out.

[35] Jesus heard that they had cast him out, and having found him he said, "Do you believe in the Son of Man?" [36] He answered, "And who is he, sir, that I may believe in him?" [37] Jesus said to him, "You have seen him, and it is he who is speaking to you." [38] He said, "Lord, I believe," and he worshiped him. [39] Jesus said, "For judgment I came into this world, that those who do not see may see, and those who see may become blind." [40] Some of the Pharisees near him heard these things, and said to him, "Are we also blind?" [41] Jesus said to them, "If you were blind, you would have no guilt; but now that you say, 'We see,' your guilt remains.

Observing the Text (verses 35-41)

What does Jesus do upon hearing the man he healed was excommunicated?

_____

_____

_____

How does the man refer to Jesus?

_____

_____

_____

Why does Jesus say he came "into the world"?

_____

_____

_____

Interpreting the Text (verses 35-41)

Why would Jesus continue the conversation with the man after healing him?

_____

_____

_____

How does this section show the essentialness of faith in Christ?

_____

_____

_____

How does Jesus use this man's lack of eyesight to teach about real blindness?

_____

_____

_____

Teaching

This lesson introduces the final element you need to craft your Grace Story: the future. Jesus is coming back. He told us he would and he is entirely faithful to his promises. One day, we will see him face to face (Revelation 22:4). When Jesus returns, it will not be to deal with our sin but to bring us into the fullness of his kingdom!

Then I saw a new heaven and a new earth, for the first heaven and the first earth had passed away, and the sea was no more. And I saw the holy city, new Jerusalem, coming down out of heaven from God, prepared as a bride adorned for her husband. And I heard a loud voice from the throne saying, "Behold, the dwelling place of God is with man. He will dwell with them, and they will be his people and God himself will be with them as their God. He will wipe away every tear from their eyes, and death shall be no more, neither shall there be mourning, nor crying, nor pain anymore, for the former things have passed away."

Revelation 21:1-4

We will have the blessed joy of being with God and his people for days without end in eternal glory—no more pain, tears, sorrow, disease, broken relationships, evil, or death. Our faith will become sight. This is what awaits every person who has placed their complete trust in Christ and his work. This is the great hope of the gospel!

This hope of Christ's return and the establishment of his kingdom should significantly impact our daily lives, especially the sorrow and hardships we face. How we view others, how we work, and how we go about life will all be transformed in light of this eternal perspective.

This hope for the future is also a powerful part of our grace story. Sadly, it's often the element of our story shared the least. This must not be so! Ephesians 2:12 teaches that everyone apart from Christ is alienated from God with no hope at all. The gospel message is the remedy. Christ not only saves us from our sin and restores us back to God, but he also secures our hope for the future. Here are some questions to get you thinking:

- How does the hope of the gospel influence your life concerning the future?

- How does the prospect of seeing Christ face to face fuel your daily worship?
- How does the promise of his return give you comfort in the midst of uncertainty and difficulty?
- When facing your own mortality, how does the gospel provide you with great security, comfort, and peace?

These questions, along with many more, should not be treated lightly. As we mature in Christ, we shouldn't seek to avoid these topics in our own lives or in conversations with others. The gospel has hope-filled answers for our most difficult questions. Spend some time today thinking about and writing out the future aspect of your Grace Story.

> He who testifies to these things says, "Surely I am coming soon." Amen. Come, Lord Jesus!
>
> Revelation 22:20

Questions for Reflection

Why do Christ followers sometimes neglect to tell the great hope of Christ's return as a part of their Grace Story?

_____

_____

_____

Do you think that in today's society it is important to be able to share about the great hope of Christ's return and how that impacts our lives? Why or why not?

_____

_____

_____

Is there someone in your life that struggles to find hope in anything, that needs to hear about the hope of Christ? How could sharing the future aspect of your Grace Story be encouraging to them?

_____

_____

_____

Prayer

Praise Jesus that he is coming again in glory and grace, bringing the restoration of his people and creation itself! Pray that he would help you to place your hope in his return and share your future Grace Story with others.

WEEKLY
EXERCISE

WRITING YOUR GRACE STORY

Write out your Grace Story using these prompts. Consider using elements from last week's Personal Salvation Story exercise for the Past Grace section. You may want to write your Grace Story on another sheet of paper. The bulleted statements are to help your thinking but by no means are they restrictive of what to write.

PAST GRACE | What was your life like before Christ?

_____

_____

_____

_____

_____

_____

_____

_____

_____

_____

_____

PRESENT GRACE | What is your life like now because of Jesus?

- *In the last six months, how has God given you comfort, direction, or hope?*
- *How has God used people to bless you?*
- *How have you seen the impact of the gospel in your marriage, home, work?*

_____

_____

_____

_____

_____

_____

_____

_____

_____

_____

_____

_____

_____

_____

FUTURE GRACE | How does the gospel impact your hopes for tomorrow?

- *How does the hope of God's ultimate redemption of all things one day move you?*
- *How does the gospel provide you with security, comfort, and peace?*
- *How does faith in Christ give us strength to embrace the unknowns of life?*

_____

_____

_____

_____

_____

_____

_____

_____

_____

_____

_____

_____

_____

Get Ready for Group

Write your memorized Scripture.

_____

_____

_____

_____

_____

What observations and interpretations of Scripture were most meaningful
to you?

_____

_____

_____

_____

Summarize your key takeaway(s) for this week.

_____

_____

_____

_____

What will you tell the group about the results of your exercise this week?

_____

_____

_____

_____

How has this week helped you better understand and apply the Spiritual Growth Grid?

_____

_____

_____

_____

_____

REPENT & BELIEVE

WHO GOD IS	WHAT GOD DID	WHO WE ARE	WHAT WE DO
KING	CALLED	CITIZENS	LISTEN & OBEY
FATHER	ADOPTED	FAMILY	LOVE & SERVE
SAVIOR	SENT	MISSIONARIES	GO & MULTIPLY

09

USING OUR GRACE STORY

SCRIPTURE MEMORY

Jesus said to him, "I am the way, and the truth, and the life. No one comes to the Father except through me."

—*John 14:6*

ENGAGING OTHERS

Scripture Study

1 CORINTHIANS 15:1-11

Now I would remind you, brothers, of the gospel I preached to you, which you received, in which you stand, ² and by which you are being saved, if you hold fast to the word I preached to you—unless you believed in vain. ³ For I delivered to you as of first importance what I also received: that Christ died for our sins in accordance with the Scriptures, ⁴ that he was buried, that he was raised on the third day in accordance with the Scriptures, ⁵ and that he appeared to Cephas, then to the twelve. ⁶ Then he appeared to more than five hundred brothers at one time, most of whom are still alive, though some have fallen asleep. ⁷ Then he appeared to James, then to all the apostles. ⁸ Last of all, as to one untimely born, he appeared also to me. ⁹ For I am the least of the apostles, unworthy to be called an apostle, because I persecuted the church of God. ¹⁰ But by the grace of God I am what I am, and his grace toward me was not in vain. On the contrary, I worked harder than any of them, though it was not I, but the grace of God that is with me. ¹¹ Whether then it was I or they, so we preach and so you believed.

Observing the Text (verses 1-2)

Where is the past, present, and future of the gospel in verses 1-2?

_____

_____

_____

How is the gospel transmitted by Paul to others?

_____

_____

_____

What must the Corinthians do in light of receiving the gospel?

_____

_____

_____

Interpreting the Text (verses 1-2)

Why does the gospel have a past, present, and future aspect to it?

_____

_____

_____

Why is it important that we can only receive the gospel and not "do" the gospel?

_____

_____

_____

What would it mean in this passage to believe in vain?

_____

_____

_____

Teaching

Every follower of Jesus has a story of redemption that is uniquely theirs, given by God as an instrument with a missional purpose. When we engage the world around us, how can we best utilize our Grace Stories so that others in our Spheres of Influence can hear that our God saves? Here are some important reminders.

First, listen. Heard this one before? We hope so. We have mentioned it multiple times in this study because it is so important. Far too often, Christians are seen as the ones who are ready to tell others what to do but refuse to listen to anyone else. Listening is key to sharing the gospel effectively! It is important to understand where others have been, what they have struggled with, and what their thoughts are about God, hope, sin, life, etc. This awareness will help us to know where our grace stories overlap with their lives.

Second, understand we may not be able to relate to the other person's situation, past, or experience on a surface level. There will be people in our Spheres of Influence with which we have a lot in common, making it easier to see how our testimony impacts them. Our shared past experiences are often easy bridges to cross, already constructed and simple to walk over. The challenge here is to actually make the intentional step to share our story with them.

But, there are other times where our story seems too far removed from the other person. It could be that their religious background is different, or their brokenness varies so much from ours that it's difficult to comprehend. They could be from a different culture, or their current situation is foreign to us (e.g., addiction, abuse, depression, dealing with loss, etc.). It may seem like our Grace Story would be meaningless to them. However, the differences, though very real, do not automatically mean God cannot work through our Grace Stories. First and foremost, our stories are about pointing others to Jesus Christ. Regardless of someone's background, culture, or experiences, the gospel message transcends all.

Finally, if you find it hard to engage someone's story with your own, remember that we all share the human effects of sin. The root problem for every person is sin. It affects every area of life. It permeates our culture, institutions, relationships, and emotions. The gospel is God's solution to sin. In Christ Jesus there is forgiveness for our sin, freedom from sin's power, and a future hope that one day sin will be gone when all things are made new. This good news is for all people!

We are all both victims of sin and willing participants in it. We must begin to look deeper than sin's short-term effects if we are going to meaningfully and faithfully share our Grace Story. The gospel is not merely about symptomatic relief but dives deep to the root problem of every man, woman, and child. If we are not careful, we can be distracted from sharing the gospel by focusing too much on symptoms of sin like addiction, insecurity, pride, or loneliness and miss the root problem the gospel addresses. As we listen to other's stories, we should ask the question, How does their story point to the ultimate problem of sin and a broken relationship with God? Our missional purpose spurs us on to give not just sympathy or advice, but a clear gospel solution. As missionaries, we must do our best to find ways to engage those in our Spheres of Influence as we share our Grace Stories, always proclaiming that the gospel is truly the good news that redeems sin's destruction in and around us.

Questions for Reflection

In what ways do you struggle to believe that God has sent you as a missionary to all those around you, even those you may not naturally connect with?

_____

_____

_____

Have you ever tried to share either your Grace Story or the gospel with someone you had difficulty relating? If so, describe your experience?

_____

_____

_____

Why is it important to share our Grace Story in a way that points to God's solution to sin and our restored relationship with God, rather than mere symptom alleviation?

_____

_____

_____

Prayer

Thank God for his great redemption that covers over all sin, regardless of our history or background. Ask him to open your eyes to opportunities to proclaim his gospel, even to those who may not seem to have much in common with you.

SCRIPTURE MEMORY

Jesus said to him, "I am the ____, and the ____, and the ___. No one comes to the Father except through me."

—*John 14:6*

THE GOSPEL AS A LENS

Scripture Study

1 CORINTHIANS 15:1-11

Now I would remind you, brothers, of the gospel I preached to you, which you received, in which you stand, ² and by which you are being saved, if you hold fast to the word I preached to you—unless you believed in vain. ³ For I delivered to you as of first importance what I also received: that Christ died for our sins in accordance with the Scriptures, ⁴ that he was buried, that he was raised on the third day in accordance with the Scriptures, ⁵ and that he appeared to Cephas, then to the twelve. ⁶ Then he appeared to more than five hundred brothers at one time, most of whom are still alive, though some have fallen asleep. ⁷ Then he appeared to James, then to all the apostles. ⁸ Last of all, as to one untimely born, he appeared also to me. ⁹ For I am the least of the apostles, unworthy to be called an apostle, because I persecuted the church of God. ¹⁰ But by the grace of God I am what I am, and his grace toward me was not in vain. On the contrary, I worked harder than any of them, though it was not I, but the grace of God that is with me. ¹¹ Whether then it was I or they, so we preach and so you believed.

Observing the text (verses 3-4)

How does Paul characterize the information about the gospel they received?

_____

_____

_____

What is the gospel message based on this passage?

_____

_____

_____

How was the work of Jesus foreknown to his listeners?

_____

_____

_____

Interpreting the text (verses 3-4)

What makes the gospel something of "first importance" to Paul?

_____

_____

_____

If Paul is going to share the gospel, what will the message consist of based on this passage?

_____

_____

_____

Why is it important to use the Scripture in sharing the gospel with others?

_____

_____

Teaching

As we listen to the experiences of those within our Spheres of Influence, we should ask the question: How does their story point to the ultimate problem of sin and a broken relationship with God? We should also look at our story with that same question in mind. It may seem that our stories are worlds apart, but all of us have the same root struggle and the same hope in Christ.

As people share their story with us, it is important to see them through the lens of the gospel, prayerfully and mindfully making connections between what we are hearing and the truths of our need for redemption through Jesus. With this lens in place, we will be able to learn what lies they believe, what roadblocks are preventing them from embracing Christ, and how their past shapes their worldview. We may also find that some of their beliefs align with what God teaches through his word. The goal is to ask questions that help move the conversation toward topics of eternal significance and listen from a gospel perspective, intent upon how their story points to the ultimate problem of sin and a broken relationship with God. Doing so processes our conversations through the gospel lens.

We then need to take the next step by asking questions:

- Does our story overlap with theirs in any way?
- Did we believe the same lies?
- Did we have similar roadblocks that hindered us from embracing the gospel?
- Do we share any past experiences of either being a victim of sin or a willing participant?
- Are they trying to earn God's favor by their own righteousness like we may have?
- Do we share any commonalities with the effects of sin that point to the

ultimate problem of it and our separation from God?

Once we begin to see the overlap (no matter how small), we can better share our story of grace. What we discover in listening to others' stories determines how we share our Grace Story.

While we've addressed this before, it's worth repeating. As missionaries, we must always remember the gospel alone addresses the deepest need for humanity. We are sinners separated from our righteous creator. However, God so loved the world that he sent Christ to live the perfect life we couldn't live and die the death we deserved. Jesus satisfied the Father's just wrath against sin as our perfect substitute. When we place our trust solely in him as Lord and Savior, we are saved by his grace, our sins are forgiven, and we are restored back into relationship with the Creator. We now experience that restored relationship with the hope of Christ's return and life together with God in a new creation. God has marked us with his Spirit who dwells within us every day. Despite what we have done or what life may throw at us, we now live with real hope!

Our grace stories should display this great truth, pointing others to the one true hope for every man, woman, and child. When we share our story in a gospel-centered way, we can lovingly challenge them to consider their lives in light of this message and the great hope it holds.
If you have been saved by Christ, 1 Peter 2:9-10 is true of you:

> But you are a chosen race, a royal priesthood, a holy nation, a people for his own possession, that you may proclaim the excellencies of him who called you out of darkness into his marvelous light. Once you were not a people, but now you are God's people; once you had not received mercy but now you have received mercy.

You belong to God. You are precious to him. You have received mercy. You have a great and powerful story to tell because it points to the ultimate story! The more you tell it, the more comfortable you will become in it. The challenge is clear.

Will we proclaim him who called us out of darkness into his marvelous light? Will we embrace the opportunity we've been given within our Spheres of Influence? Will we share our story so others can see and hear the gospel of Jesus Christ as well? Missionaries say, "Yes! Send us!"

Questions for Reflection

Why is it important to see other people's stories through the lens of the gospel?

_____

_____

_____

Do you agree that all people have the same ultimate need, to be saved from their sin and restored back into relationship with God? Why or why not?

_____

_____

_____

With whom do you want to share your Grace Story? Do you feel equipped to share in a gospel centered way? Why or why not? What would help you feel more equipped?

_____

_____

_____

Prayer

Ask God to help you to see those in your Spheres of Influence through the lens of the gospel, connecting their experiences and struggles with the deeper need for salvation. Pray that he would speak through you as you share your Grace Story with them.

SCRIPTURE MEMORY

_____ said to him, "I am the way, and the truth, and the life. _____ comes to the _____ except through me."

—*John 14:6*

TIME TO PROCESS

Scripture Study

1 CORINTHIANS 15:1-11

Now I would remind you, brothers, of the gospel I preached to you, which you received, in which you stand, ² and by which you are being saved, if you hold fast to the word I preached to you—unless you believed in vain. ³For I delivered to you as of first importance what I also received: that Christ died for our sins in accordance with the Scriptures, ⁴ that he was buried, that he was raised on the third day in accordance with the Scriptures, ⁵and that he appeared to Cephas, then to the twelve. ⁶ Then he appeared to more than five hundred brothers at one time, most of whom are still alive, though some have fallen asleep. ⁷ Then he appeared to James, then to all the apostles. ⁸ Last of all, as to one untimely born, he appeared also to me. ⁹ For I am the least of the apostles, unworthy to be called an apostle, because I persecuted the church of God. ¹⁰ But by the grace of God I am what I am, and his grace toward me was not in vain. On the contrary, I worked harder than any of them, though it was not I, but the grace of God that is with me. ¹¹ Whether then it was I or they, so we preach and so you believed.

Observing the Text (verses 5-11)

To whom does Paul say the resurrected Christ appeared?

How does Paul describe his apostleship?

What is the agency through which the Corinthians believed based on verse 11?

Interpreting the Text (verses 5-11)

Why would Paul cite the names of people who saw the resurrected Christ?

Why is it important for Paul to tell the Corinthians concerning his apostolic ministry that "by the grace of God I am what I am"? What does this tell us about our identity as missionaries?

Why is preaching (declaring the person and work of God in Christ) so critical in the sharing of the gospel?

_____

_____

_____

How does 1 Corinthians 12 impact your thoughts about your role in the body of Christ? Do you know what function God has given you?

_____

_____

_____

Teaching

In 1960, the Big Texan Steak Ranch opened its doors on the roadside of the famous Route 66. One evening a hungry cowboy ventured in, bragging that he was so hungry that he could "eat the whole, darned cow." R.J. "Bob" Lee, the Big Texan's founder, started cooking him steaks. When the cowpoke finally hollered "calf rope" (signifying he was done), he had consumed four-and-a-half pounds of delicious Texas beef. Bob Lee vowed from that day forward the steak dinner would be served free to anyone who could consume it in one hour. My father, who grew up in Amarillo, told me that, not only do you have to eat the steak in an hour, but also all the sides (a salad, a potato, and a roll) included with it. For most of us, the steak itself would be an overwhelming task.

The "Free 72-ounce Steak Dinner" is still flourishing at the Big Texan. More than 40,000 people have attempted to consume the prized meal since 1960, and about 7,000 have succeeded. People from all over the world continue to visit the restaurant to take the challenge and claim the bragging rights. Pro Wrestler Klondike Bill ate two in an hour back in the 1960s, while the quickest anyone finished was in nine-and-a-half minutes!

I asked someone who tried their hand at a similar meal how they approached such a grand feat. They replied, "One bite at a time." That's good advice. Trying to consume something so big should be done properly and in good order. A failure to do so would have you winding up either very sick or very dead.

Responding to the gospel, much like the challenge of a 72-ounce steak, is an enormous endeavor. The gospel makes demands, calls for commitment, asks for faith, and ultimately seeks the life of the one who wants to receive it. Those big issues should cause most people to deeply ponder the implications of it all. Jesus understood that. In Luke 14:28-30, he compares someone becoming his disciple to a person about to engage in the enterprise of a big construction project:

> For which of you, desiring to build a tower, does not first sit down and count the cost, whether he has enough to complete it? Otherwise, when he has laid a foundation and is not able to finish, all who see it begin to mock him, saying, "This man began to build and was not able to finish."

It's very clear. A wise person will take time to consider the cost of committing to something, especially something that will cost him a great deal. Only a foolish person begins such a large undertaking without thinking about whether or not he can finish it.

That truth should help temper our possible impatience with others as we share the gospel. Not everyone after hearing the offer of Jesus will immediately walk down an aisle or pray a prayer to receive Christ. Most want to think about who Jesus is, what he has done, and how that intersects with them. For many, doing so takes time. It can take weeks, months, or even years before a person is ready to give their heart and life to Jesus. So, when we share the gospel, as missionaries we must remember that most people within our Spheres of Influence will need time to process the weightiness and implications of what Jesus has done.

No one in their right mind would try to swallow a steak whole. You must take it bite by bite. Most people can't swallow everything the gospel entails in one big chunk; they must take it bite by bite. Let that truth fuel your patience with those you're trying to reach who are far from God. Keep sharing your Grace Story, keep presenting the gospel, and keep inviting them into your gospel community at your local campus. You never know— you may find that the person is on their last bite!

Everyone has something to offer. You build the sense of connection and value for each other as you encourage and celebrate everyone giving and serving the way God created them to give and serve. You belong, and so do they.

Questions for Reflection

How long did it take you to consider the claims of Jesus before you crossed the line of faith? How did other believers respond who walked with you through that decision?

_____

_____

_____

How does it feel knowing that most people need time to process the call of the gospel on their lives? How does that affect your sharing with them?

_____

_____

_____

What issues or areas of the gospel do you think would cause a person to deeply ponder their commitment to them?

_____

_____

_____

Prayer

Thank God for his patience with each one of us as he lovingly drew us to himself, whether that took years or moments. Pray that he would give you the patience to faithfully share your Grace Story with those in your Spheres of Influence, no matter how long it takes.

WEEKLY EXERCISE

———

SHARE YOUR GRACE STORY

Individual with whom you shared your story:

_____

Debrief Questions:

What was it like to share your Grace Story with others?

_____
_____
_____
_____
_____
_____
_____

Did you feel confident in sharing your story after telling it several times?

_____
_____
_____
_____
_____
_____
_____

Did you feel equipped to articulate the gospel? Why or why not?

_____
_____
_____
_____
_____
_____

What can you do to continue building confidence in sharing your Grace Story and articulating the gospel??

_____

_____

_____

_____

_____

_____

_____

Get Ready for Group

Write your memorized Scripture.

_____

_____

_____

_____

_____

What observations and interpretations of Scripture were most meaningful to you?

_____

_____

_____

_____

_____

Summarize your key takeaway(s) for this week.

_____

_____

_____

_____

_____

What will you tell the group about the results of your exercise this week?

_____

_____

_____

_____

_____

How has this week helped you better understand and apply the Spiritual Growth Grid?

_____

_____

_____

_____

_____

REPENT & BELIEVE

WHO GOD IS	WHAT GOD DID	WHO WE ARE	WHAT WE DO
KING	CALLED	CITIZENS	LISTEN & OBEY
FATHER	ADOPTED	FAMILY	LOVE & SERVE
SAVIOR	SENT	MISSIONARIES	GO & MULTIPLY

10

SHARING WISELY

SCRIPTURE MEMORY

Jesus said to him, "I am the way, and the truth, and the life. No one comes to the Father except through me."

—*John 14:6*

HELPS ON SHARING YOUR STORY

Scripture Study

2 CORINTHIANS 2:12-17

When I came to Troas to preach the gospel of Christ, even though a door was opened for me in the Lord, [13] my spirit was not at rest because I did not find my brother Titus there. So I took leave of them and went on to Macedonia.

[14] But thanks be to God, who in Christ always leads us in triumphal procession, and through us spreads the fragrance of the knowledge of him everywhere. [15] For we are the aroma of Christ to God among those who are being saved and among those who are perishing, [16] to one a fragrance from death to death, to the other a fragrance from life to life. Who is sufficient for these things? [17] For we are not, like so many, peddlers of God's word, but as men of sincerity, as commissioned by God, in the sight of God we speak in Christ.

Observing the Text (verses 12-13)

What was the reason Paul travelled to Troas?

_____

_____

_____

What does Paul say the Lord did for him there?

_____

_____

_____

What is the result of Paul surveying the situation in Troas?

_____

_____

_____

Interpreting the Text (verses 12-13)

What does it mean for Paul to have "a door opened for [him] in the Lord"?

_____

_____

_____

What does that tell us about preaching the gospel and the providential hand of God?

_____

_____

_____

What could be the importance of Paul wanting Titus with him?

_____

_____

_____

Teaching

Ask any advertising executive the most powerful way to promote an idea, person, or product, and they'll all have the same answer: *word of mouth.*

Word-of-mouth marketing elevates movies to blockbuster status, turns relatively insignificant toys into the "must buy" for the holiday season, and helps restaurants consistently fill to capacity (or warns potential patrons to stay away). Personal stories carry great weight with listeners. Hearing about someone's interaction with a movie, toy, or eating establishment does much more for us than any corporate advertisement or review in the paper.

That same dynamic applies to sharing the message of Jesus Christ. When we speak to others about how Jesus has intersected with our own lives, it seems to have a very big sway in the thoughts and minds of the listener. Let's look at Mark 5:1-20.

They came to the other side of the sea, to the country of the Gerasenes. And when Jesus had stepped out of the boat, immediately there met him out of the tombs a man with an unclean spirit. He lived among the tombs. And no one could bind him anymore, not even with a chain, for he had often been bound with shackles and chains, but he wrenched the chains apart, and he broke the shackles in pieces. No one had the strength to subdue him. Night and day among the tombs and on the mountains he was always crying out and cutting himself with stones. And when he saw Jesus from afar, he ran and fell down before him. And crying out with a loud voice, he said, "What have you to do with me, Jesus, Son of the Most High God? I adjure you by God, do not torment me." For he was saying to him, "Come out of the man, you unclean spirit!" And Jesus asked him, "What is your name?" He replied, "My name is Legion, for we are many." And he begged him earnestly not to send them out of the country. Now a great herd of pigs was feeding there on the hillside, and they begged him, saying, "Send us to the pigs; let us enter them." So he gave them permission. And the unclean spirits came out and entered the pigs; and the herd, numbering about two thousand, rushed down the steep bank into the sea and drowned in the sea.

The herdsmen fled and told it in the city and in the country. And people came to see what it was that had happened. And they came to Jesus and saw the demon-possessed man, the one who had had the legion, sitting there, clothed and in his right mind, and they were afraid. And those who had seen it described to them what had happened to the demon-possessed man and to the pigs. And they began to beg Jesus to depart from their region. As he was getting into the boat, the man who had been possessed with demons begged him that he might be with him. And he did not permit him but said to him, "Go home to your friends and tell them how much the Lord has done for you, and how he has had mercy on you." And he went away and began to proclaim in the Decapolis how much Jesus had done for him, and everyone marveled.

Jesus rescues a man who is tormented in both body and soul. As the story closes, we find Christ departing from the region and the healed man begging that he might go with Jesus. That's certainly understandable. If you had been rescued from these horrific experiences, wouldn't you want to remain with your deliverer? Yet in the midst of this grateful man's request to stay, Jesus gives him an unexpected response:

And he did not permit him but said to him,"Go home to your friends and tell them how much the Lord has done for you, and how he has had mercy on you."

Mark 5:19

Jesus tells him to go back to his home and tell his friends about what God did for him. What a powerful thought! In Jesus' mind, it was more important that this man go to his friends and tell them his Grace Story than to physically stay with Jesus as he continued his ministry. Sharing your story about what Jesus has done for you must be a pretty big deal. Word of mouth proclamation concerning how the gospel has impacted us is a powerful tool God used during the days of the New Testament, and one he still uses today.

Here are a few practical things to keep in mind when it comes to sharing your Grace Story with those in your Spheres of Influence:

- **Be Brief** – Too much information, too quickly, may overload the listener. Find the balance between brevity and making sure that you've appropriately gotten to the truth of who Jesus is and what he has done for you.

- **Be Basic** – Make your story clear to your listener by avoiding church clichés or theological language they may not understand. For example, it might be hard for the listener to open up when you ask, "Did you know that Jesus' substitutionary atonement justified me and is sanctifying me today?"

- **Be Bold** – You would be surprised how many people want to hear about your spiritual journey. It may be through your story that they can begin to grasp the idea that they need Christ. Take a chance!

Think about your Spheres of Influence. Who can you impact as you "go home to your friends and tell them how much the Lord has done for you, and how he has had mercy on you"? What would you share with them? How would you do it? When might the opportunity present itself? What language would you need to use in order to best connect with them? These are the types of questions missionaries work through in order to best share the gospel.

Questions for Reflection

How have you experienced the power of word-of-mouth communication? What have you tried or believed based on the witness of someone else— from small to serious examples?

_____

_____

_____

What is the difference between being basic as opposed to being overly simplistic? What does this look like in practice?

_____

_____

_____

What is your biggest fear about being bold to share?

_____

_____

_____

Prayer

Thank God for those that he has placed within your Spheres of Influence and for the opportunity to join him in his mission to save them. Pray that God would help you to share your Grace Story boldly.

SCRIPTURE MEMORY

Jesus said to him, "I am _____, and

_____, and _____. No one comes

to the Father _____."

—John 14:6

OUR ROLE, GOD'S ROLE

Scripture Study

2 CORINTHIANS 2:12-17

When I came to Troas to preach the gospel of Christ, even though a door was opened for me in the Lord, [13] my spirit was not at rest because I did not find my brother Titus there. So I took leave of them and went on to Macedonia.

[14] But thanks be to God, who in Christ always leads us in triumphal procession, and through us spreads the fragrance of the knowledge of him everywhere. [15] For we are the aroma of Christ to God among those who are being saved and among those who are perishing, [16] to one a fragrance from death to death, to the other a fragrance from life to life. Who is sufficient for these things? [17] For we are not, like so many, peddlers of God's word, but as men of sincerity, as commissioned by God, in the sight of God we speak in Christ.

Observing the text (verses 14-15)

What is Paul's first response to this situation in verse 14?

How does he refer to the gospel presence of believers in the world?

Who is this "aroma" for based on verses 14-15?

Interpreting the text (verses 14-15)

What does it mean that God "always leads us in triumphal procession" in Christ?

Why would someone's gospel presence be described as "the aroma of Christ"?

How does the aroma of Christ spread itself "through us"?

Teaching

An important truth, which can help missionaries to share wisely, is knowing the difference between our role and God's role. Evangelism is actually the enactment of divine cooperation where both God and human beings are at work to share the gospel. How so? Let's look back at Lydia's story in Acts 16:13-15, where Paul the Apostle and his church planting team finds a group of devout Jewish women gathered outside Philippi to study the Scriptures:

> *And on the Sabbath day we went outside the gate to the riverside, where we supposed there was a place of prayer, and we sat down and spoke to the women who had come together. One who heard us was a woman named Lydia, from the city of Thyatira, a seller of purple goods, who was a worshiper of God. The Lord opened her heart to pay attention to what was said by Paul. And after she was baptized, and her household as well, she urged us, saying, "If you have judged me to be faithful to the Lord, come to my house and stay." And she prevailed upon us.*

Why did Lydia believe? Was she smarter, stronger, or more religious than the others around her? The Bible simply says that "the Lord opened her heart." God changed her from inside to make her someone she could not be on her own. In other words, when it came to her salvation, God made the first move. He moved on the inside. She responded on the outside. If that seems confusing, don't worry! This is a great mystery between God and man.

But there was another essential piece to this work: Paul spoke about Jesus. Paul was faithful to share the gospel and God was faithful to enable Lydia to respond by faith to the gospel. This is why evangelism is where both man and God are at work. Our job is to share. God's job is to save.

This truth is incredibly freeing for missionaries who are called to share the gospel in word and deed. It means we don't have to guilt trip, manipulate, or twist others' arms to get them to embrace Jesus. Missionaries know their biggest goal is to share the gospel clearly, sincerely, and lovingly. We can leave the results up to God. He alone is the one who demolishes the barriers of the heart, removes the hurdles of disbelief, and brings to life that which is dead.

This also means missionaries don't need to feel devastated when others reject the sharing of their Grace Story. Conversely, it means they shouldn't feel cocky or boastful if others receive their Grace Story as well. We are not the agent of change—God is. May this wonderful truth give us deeper confidence in sharing the gospel, drive us to our knees in prayer with greater frequency and fervency, and cause us to gladly praise God when we see other hearts opened to receive the gospel we share, knowing that the Lord is at work!

Questions for Reflection

How can we get greater confidence in sharing the gospel knowing the difference between our role and God's role in evangelism?

_____

_____

_____

How can pressure to "make a decision happen" lead us into bad practices as missionaries within our Spheres of Influence?

_____

_____

_____

SHARING THE GOSPEL **IN WORD AND DEED**

How can we balance feeling a deep responsibility to those within our Spheres of Influence and trusting in God to accomplish their salvation?

_____

_____

_____

Prayer

Praise God for his great work in opening your heart to believe the gospel, moving inside you so that you might respond in faith. Pray for those within your Spheres of Influence, that God's work within would be preparing their hearts to hear your Grace Story.

SCRIPTURE MEMORY

_____, "I am the way, and the truth, and the life. _____ _____ except through me."

—*John 14:6*

REMEMBER YOUR IDENTITY: A RECAP

Scripture Study

2 CORINTHIANS 2:12-17

When I came to Troas to preach the gospel of Christ, even though a door was opened for me in the Lord, *13* my spirit was not at rest because I did not find my brother Titus there. So I took leave of them and went on to Macedonia.

14 But thanks be to God, who in Christ always leads us in triumphal procession, and through us spreads the fragrance of the knowledge of him everywhere. *15* For we are the aroma of Christ to God among those who are being saved and among those who are perishing, *16* to one a fragrance from death to death, to the other a fragrance from life to life. Who is sufficient for these things? *17* For we are not, like so many, peddlers of God's word, but as men of sincerity, as commissioned by God, in the sight of God we speak in Christ.

Observing the Text (verses 16-17)

How does this aroma impact those around it?

_____

_____

_____

What is the contrast given in verse 17?

_____

_____

_____

How are "men of sincerity" described?

_____

_____

_____

Interpreting the Text (verses 16-17)

What does it mean to be a fragrance of death to death to some and a fragrance of life to life with others?

_____

_____

_____

How does some become a "peddler of God's word"?

_____

_____

_____

Why is it important to see our gospel mission as a commissioning of God and done before God?

_____

Teaching

This 10-week study was designed to better help us share the gospel in word and display its power by deed, fulfilling our new purpose given to us as followers of Jesus. For our final lesson, we want to recap why this purpose and these activities are to be true of us and evient in our lives. As we noted in the primer on gospel-centered discipleship, there is a gospel order to growth:

Identity Informs Activity

Who we are determines what we do. Our identity as believers—those who have been raised with Christ and whose lives are hidden with Christ in God—is the determining factor at the root of our activity. It is *why* we seek to set our minds on the things that are above. As it concerns who God is, what he did in Christ, and how that impacts us, each week has consistently pointed to a specific storyline:

WHO GOD IS	WHAT GOD DID	WHO WE ARE	WHAT WE DO
SAVIOR	SENTM	ISSIONARIES	GO & MULTIPLY

God the Father sent Jesus to be our Savior, but he was not finished sending. As followers of Christ, we also are sent into our world to proclaim that God has come to redeem and restore people and, ultimately, all things back to God. We call sent people *missionaries*. This role is given to all believers in the gospel. Once again, it is a part of our gospel identity. It is also why the activity of going and multiplying (e.g., the work of missional living) is a normal and expected aspect of the Christian life. This is our new gospel-given purpose in life.

Read again to Corinthians 5:17-21, the passage we examined in Week 1:

> *Therefore, if anyone is in Christ, he is a new creation. The old has passed away; behold, the new has come. All this is from God, who through Christ reconciled us to himself and gave us the ministry of reconciliation; that is, in Christ God was reconciling the world to himself, not counting their trespasses against them, and entrusting to us the message of reconciliation. Therefore, we are ambassadors for Christ, God making his appeal through us. We implore you on behalf of Christ, be reconciled to God.*

We are reconcilers because, in Christ, we have been reconciled. Identity informs activity! God makes his children a missionary people.

Putting it all together, we can say the mission of the church is to participate in God's rescue work by *going* into the world declaring the gospel in word and demonstrating its power in deed in the hopes that followers of Jesus will be *multiplied* as a result. This specific study has sought to train followers of Jesus on sharing God's gospel. But training is of little help if, in the long run, we miss the foundational truth that what we do for Christ is rooted in who we are in Christ. May we grow deeply as disciple-making disciples by leading the way, living out our new purpose through a missional life that shares the gospel in word and displays its power in deed!

Questions for Reflection

How has this study deepened your identity in Jesus?

_____

_____

_____

Why is it important for followers of Jesus to understand their gospel identity?

_____

_____

_____

How can the gospel order of "identity before activity" make a big difference in how a disciple obeys God, specifically related to missional living?

_____

_____

_____

Prayer

Thank God for the power of the gospel of Jesus to accomplish his great work of redemption and pray that he would strengthen your faith as you participate in his mission of making disciples.

WEEKLY EXERCISE

MISSIONAL STRATEGY

Take some time this week to work on a missional strategy for how to begin engaging your Spheres of Influence. Refer to the activity from session one where you identified those within your spheres of influence, as well as the activities listed in session two. Use the guide below as a starting point to help you plan out your next steps.

ACTIVITY	NON-BELIEVER	BELIEVER	NEXT STEP
ACTIVITY	NON-BELIEVER	BELIEVER	NEXT STEP
ACTIVITY	NON-BELIEVER	BELIEVER	NEXT STEP
ACTIVITY	NON-BELIEVER	BELIEVER	NEXT STEP

Get Ready for Group

Write your memorized Scripture.

_____

_____

_____

_____

_____

What observations and interpretations of Scripture were most meaningful to you?

_____

_____

_____

_____

_____

Summarize your key takeaway(s) for this week.

_____

_____

_____

_____

_____

What will you tell the group about the results of your exercise this week?

_____

_____

_____

_____

_____

How has this week helped you better understand and apply the Spiritual Growth Grid?

_____

_____

_____

_____

_____

REPENT & BELIEVE			
WHO GOD IS	WHAT GOD DID	WHO WE ARE	WHAT WE DO
KING	CALLED	CITIZENS	LISTEN & OBEY
FATHER	ADOPTED	FAMILY	LOVE & SERVE
SAVIOR	SENT	MISSIONARIES	GO & MULTIPLY

Made in the USA
Monee, IL
10 June 2020